# GARLAND OF DIVINE FLOWERS

# Garland of Divine Flowers

*Selected Devotional Lyrics of*
SAINT JÑĀNEŚVARA

P.V. BOBDE

*With a foreword by*
P.N. JOSHI

MOTILAL BANARSIDASS PUBLISHERS
PRIVATE LIMITED • DELHI

*First Edition: Delhi, 1987*
*Reprint: Delhi, 1995, 1999*



ISBN: 81-208-0400-7

*Also available at:*

MOTILAL BANARSIDASS

41 U.A. Bungalow Road, Jawahar Nagar, Delhi 110 007
8 Mahalaxmi Chamber, Warden Road, Mumbai 400 026
120 Royapettah High Road, Mylapore, Chennai 600 004
Sanas Plaza, 1302 Baji Rao Road, Pune 411 002
16 St. Mark's Road, Bangalore 560 001
8 Camac Street, Calcutta 700 017
Ashok Rajpath, Patna 800 004
Chowk, Varanasi 221 001

PRINTED IN INDIA
BY JAINENDRA PRAKASH JAIN AT SHRI JAINENDRA PRESS,
A-45 NARAINA, PHASE I, NEW DELHI 110 028
AND PUBLISHED BY NARENDRA PRAKASH JAIN FOR
MOTILAL BANARSIDASS PUBLISHERS PRIVATE LIMITED,
BUNGALOW ROAD, DELHI 110 007

*To the Sacred Memory of*

SAINT JÑĀNEŚVARA

*"There are numerous eye-like spots on the plumage of a peacock, but these are of no use as they lack vision. Similarly, empty clouds fleeting across the sky are of no avail. All your actions are likewise fruitless unless you worship Śrī Kṛṣṇa, the Protector of Gokula."*

SAINT JÑĀNEŚVARA

# FOREWORD

I have great pleasure in writing a foreword to the book, *Garland of Divine Flowers: Selected Devotional Lyrics of Saint Jñāneśvara* of Sri P. V. Bobde. Sri Bobde has got a great reverence for Marathi saints and their literature and is a devoted and authoritative student of their philosophy and mystic life. Readers are already well acquainted with his devotional and poetic mind as reflected in his book of poems—*At Thy Feet*. In presenting this book of his lyrical poems, reminiscent of Ravindranath Tagore's *Gitanjali*, to the readers having a spiritual leaning, he has established his authority in this field.

The spiritual life and the devotional lyrics of Saint Jñāneśvara and other Marathi saints still continue to have their spell on the minds of the people. Saint Jñāneśvara who belonged to the thirteenth century, besides being famous as a great saint, philosopher and poet is also known and respected as an expert organiser of 'Bhakti-Mārga'. In his life-time saints like Nāmadeva, Narahari (goldsmith), Sāvatā (gardener), Senā (barber), Gorobā (potter), Cokhāmelā and others sprang up from various castes and strata of society and attained spiritual equality at the door of the Lord. Though Śrī Jñāneśvara's *Jñāneśvarī* or *Bhāvārtha-Dīpikā,* a philosophical treatise, is reputed as an elucidation of or a commentary on *Bhagavadgītā*, his emotional aptitude and highly poetical style have made his philosophy most enlivening. His another work *Anubhavāmṛta* based on his spiritual revelations is a rare combination of philosophy and poetic imagery. His *Cāngadeva Pāsaṣtī* contains a gist of his philosophy as expounded in both these works. In his one thousand and odd stray Abhaṅgas, Śrī Jñāneśvara has vividly depicted his experiences of the grand union between 'Jīva' and 'Śiva' and 'Ātman' and 'Paramātman'.

The influence which these towering literary works of Śrī Jñāneśvara wield over the popular mind and the cultural life of Maharashtra is remarkably great even today. Saints like Nāmadeva, Ekanātha, Tukārāma, Nilobā, Bahiṇābaī and others have popularised like a highway the footpath of 'Bhakti-Mārga' trodden by Śrī Jñāneśvara. What is the greatest happiness in a man's life? The appeal of Śrī Jñāneśvara's poetic literature which endeavours to provide a correct answer to this question is not limited only to the Marathi-speaking people. There is a great spell of this devotional poetry on the readers in the other Indian languages and the languages of the world as well. Those acquainted with this field of literature are aware of the attempts made by Justine E. Abbott, Manu Subhedar, R.D. Ranade, N.R. Godbole, R.K. Bhagwat, Pradhan and Lambert and other Indian and foreign scholars for translating *Śrī Jñāneśvarī* into English. Sri Vitthala Ganesh Pradhan had translated the entire *Jñāneśvarī* in a simple and easy English prose The Unesco, an international organisation, has published in the years 1967 and 1969 the English translation of *Jñāneśvarī* in two volumes which Miss Lambert had done by improving upon the translation of Sri Pradhan. Sri B.P. Bahirat of Pandharpura who is a scholar of the literary works of the saints has included at the end of his book, *The Philosophy of Jñānadeva* a complete prose rendering in English of Śrī Jñāneśvara's *Anubhavāmṛta.* In the second edition of this book published in 1961, Sri Bahirat has included the English translation of a few Abhaṅgas of Śrī Jñāneśvara as specimens. Earlier, R.D. Ranade in his celebrated work *Mysticism in Maharashtra* while describing the world of the mystic experiences of Śrī Jñāneśvara has translated some of his Abhaṅgas. The oldest attempt to translate Śrī Jñāneśvara's Abhaṅgas into English, it appears, was made by Dr. Nikol Macnical in the year 1919. This European scholar, who collaborated with Rev. Abbott in his work, *The Psalms of Maratha Saints* has introduced the poems of Maratha saints to his English readers. Though out of these one hundred and eight Abhaṅgas a major portion is devoted to the Abhaṅgas of Ekanātha and Tukārāma, a few Abhaṅgas of Jñāneśvara, Janābāī, Muktābāī, Nāmadeva and others also find place in this compilation. The first page of this book speaks of this collection as a rosary of 108 Tulsi beads (A rosary of Tulsi Beads for Helen and France). In this context Mr. Macnical's article "The Indian Poetry of Devotion" deserves mention.

On this background Sri Bobde's book of translation of Śrī Jñāneśvara's selected Abhaṅgas is especially valuable and praiseworthy. Out of Śrī Jñāneśvara's one thousand and odd Abhaṅgas he has very aptly and judiciously selected one hundred and ten Abhaṅgas and rendering them into a simple and beautiful English has introduced them to the English-knowing readers. It is for the first time that the English-knowing readers are being acquainted with the world of mystic experiences of Śrī Jñāneśvara as revealed in his Abhaṅgas on such a wide scale. Abhaṅga is a precious ornament of the old Marathi poetry of the saints. Metaphysics is discussed in a treatise or a thesis. On the other hand, communion or converse held with God is given vent to through stray lyrics, the Abhaṅgas. The affinity established by the self with the universal self is an experience too difficult to be expressed in words. This mystic experience is ineffable. It is like the experience of a dumb tasting sugar but not being able to describe in words its sweetness. Saint Tukārāma also says the same thing when he says that love can only be felt but cannot be expressed in words. Viewed on this background, great saints like Jñāneśvara have done a signal and valuable service to posterity for their prosperity, happiness and spiritual contentment by expressing their mystic and exquisite poetic experiences through the medium of words. Looked at from this point of view, Marathi Abhaṅga is not only a form of metre but could be treated as a kind of aptitude too.

It is really an uphill task to translate in a foreign language these Abhaṅgas which have emanated from the highly mystic experiences of the Maratha saints. Firstly, a person has to understand the true import of the deep mystic experience vividly expressed by the saints but too difficult to be put into words, then, he has to identify which particular tinge of devotion is indicated in the stray Abhaṅga and after due meditation has finally to translate it into English, meticulously following the old usages, spiritual enigma and the symbolic language. This demands a special type of calibre. A mere knowledge of the Marathi or the English language would not suffice for this purpose. It is necessary for one to have a close acquaintance with the Maratha culture.

teachings of the saints and the customs of the people. It is well-nigh impossible to translate into another language popular customs or special idioms peculiar to a language.

In the circumstances we cannot do better than approach the true import as near as possible. "पैल तो गे काऊ कोकताहे" (Paila to ge kāū kokatāhe) is Śrī Jñāneśvara's excellent and beautiful poem. It depicts the restless mental state of a man eagerly waiting for the realisation of God. He says "पैल तो गे काऊ कोकताहे" (Paila to ge kāū kokatāhe) 'A crow on the tree in the courtyard is cawing since morning.' In the cultural life of Maharashtra, this presage, suggestive of the arrival of a dear guest, is being considered as a good omen from historical times. The otherwise ill-omened crow comes into the yard, caws and suggests the happy news of the arrival of a dear one. Unless a person has knowledge of this symbol which is nowadays falling into oblivion, he would not be able to grasp the real import of the English translation reading as—'A crow has started cawing on the yonder side of the house.' Sri Bobde has made a good attempt to elucidate this symbol on the strength of his proficiency in translation and accurate insight. Though the translator has attempted to explain the meaning of some symbols in the Glossary appearing at the end of the book, I think, if explanatory notes along with the meaning of Abhaṅgas are given instead of indicating the bare meaning of the Maratha folk life, figurative symbols and significant idioms, it would be more helpful to the English-knowing readers to understand the importance of the innermost emotions of Śrī Jñāneśvara. Else, how can the reader understand the 'Virahiṇī form' of poetry?

The selection of Abhaṅgas made by Sri Bobde for the purpose of translation is very thoughtful and appropriate. Sri Bobde's translation enables the readers to have a panoramic view of a number of important and varied subjects such as description of the infatuating Saguṇa form of the Lord, His Saguṇa-Nirguṇa attributes, the glory of His name, Lord Pāṇḍuraṅga or Viṭṭhala of Paṇḍharī, greatness of saints, nature of self-realisation, advice to seekers of spiritual knowledge, etc. Lord Viṭṭhala of Paṇḍharī is the most revered deity of the Maratha saints. Sri Bobde has provided to his English readers a very fine and lively company of numerous experiences of the alluring Saguṇa form of Lord Viṭṭhala, the glory of His name, yearning and the restlessness of mind felt by a devotee on His separation, His constant remembrance, the ultimate happy realisation, etc., for which he cannot be adequately thanked.

One most important and significant Abhaṅga of Śrī Jñāneśvara begins with the line "इवलेसें रोप लाविलें द्वारीं । (Ivalese ropa lāvile dvārī) and ends with "मनाचिये गुंती गुंफियेला शेला । बाप रखुमादेविवरु विठ्ठलीं अर्पिला ॥ (Manāciye guntī guṁphiyelā śelā Bāpa Rakhumādevīvaru Viṭṭhalī arpilā). 'I have planted this small seedling of devotion at my door. This seedling, this Mogarā creeper has yielded numerous beautiful flowers of the import of devotion. This creeper laden with beautiful and fragrant flowers of Ātman-principle has grown so high as to touch the very sky.' While describing the nature of this creeper of spirituality, Sri Bobde has said, 'I wove them (flowers) into a beautiful garland and offered it to the Lord of Rakhumāī, father Viṭṭhala.' Taking a clue of these sentiments of Śrī Jñāneśvara, it can be said that Sri Bobde has rendered a great service to the English-knowing readers by preparing a garland of one hundred and ten beautiful and fragrant flowers of Śrī Jñāneśvara's inmost feelings. I humbly pray at the feet of Śrī Viṭṭhala and Śrī Jñāneśvara that Sri Bobde, who possesses a sentimental mind may get an opportunity to add to this wreath numerous other flowers of his poems.

P.N. JOSHI

# PREFACE

I feel great pleasure in presenting to the readers this English translation of some of the selected devotional lyrics of Śrī Jñāneśvara (or Jñānadeva) the greatest poet-saint of Maharashtra. It is he who laid the foundation of the 'Bhāgavata Dharma'—the path of devotion in Maharashtra. He is mostly known for his immortal classic, his Marathi commentary, *Jñāneśvarī* on the *Bhagavadgītā* translations of which are available in Hindi and English. People outside Maharashtra, however, are not much acquainted with his devotional lyrics (Abhaṅgas) as these have not been translated either into Hindi or English. The present English translation is, therefore, an attempt in that direction.

The Abhaṅgas of Śrī Jñāneśvara are the outpourings of his heart especially in the matter of relation of the soul to God. Though they cover a wide variety of subjects including his reflection on and criticism of social customs, the main purpose of his Abhaṅgas is to express the innermost feelings of his heart. The credit of being the first great writer of Abhaṅga literature also goes to him.

There are in all 1 100 Abhaṅgas to his credit. It would be a stupendous task to translate them all. I have, therefore, selected only 110 Abhaṅgas which, in my opinion, are representative of his entire Abhaṅgas. The selected Abhaṅgas have been culled from the Marathi book *Sārtha Jñānadeva Abhaṅga Gāthā* edited by Dr. P.N. Joshi, who is a great scholar of the literature pertaining to Maratha saints. While translating the Abhaṅgas, I have generally followed the Marathi meaning of the Abhaṅgas as given in the said Gāthā. An attempt has been made to render religious expressions by the nearest English equivalents. So far as the translation of Abhaṅgas is concerned, I would like to clarify that it is not literal, but attempts to explain their purport as fully as possible.

*Gaulaṇī* (*Gopīs*) *and Virahiṇī Abhaṅgas*

Some of Śrī Jñāneśvara's Abhaṅgas are known as 'Gaulaṇī-

Virahiṇī" Abhaṅgas which are spiritually allegorical in nature. In the former, he describes the intense love of the Gopīs for Lord Kṛṣṇa to give vent to his own feelings of deep devotion to God.

In the latter type, viz. 'Virahiṇī Abhaṅgas' he echoes the sentiments of a beloved pining after her separated lover to depict his intense craving for God's early 'Darśana'.

Both these types of Abhaṅgas occupy a special place in the Abhaṅgas of Śrī Jñāneśvara as poetically they are exquisite and from the devotional and philosophical standpoint are of a high order. In fact, in some of these Abhaṅgas Śrī Jñāneśvara is found to be at his best.

*Śrī Jñāneśvara's mystic experiences*

The world of Śrī Jñāneśvara's mystic experience is very rich and vivid. A mystic is supposed to see some special colours and to experience certain lights, sounds, etc. Śrī Jñāneśvara has described all these experiences through a number of his Abhaṅgas. Readers will come across a few of such type of Abhaṅgas in this collection.

The Abhaṅgas are serially numbered. The number in the bracket appearing at the end of each Abhaṅga relates to the number of the corresponding Marathi Abhaṅga in Dr. Joshi's volume. This has been done with a view to facilitating the readers' referring to the original Marathi Abhaṅga which has been translated. A glossary of Sanskrit and Marathi words together with their English equivalents is also appended.

A short life-sketch of Śrī Jñāneśvara based on the one appearing in Dr. Joshi's *Abhaṅga Gāthā* has also been included in the present book for information of the readers.

This book is mainly intended for those readers who are not acquainted with the Marathi language. It is hoped, the present work would give them an idea of Śrī Jñāneśvara's Abhaṅgas in general and would also divulge to them the richness of his thoughts and the depth of his mystic experiences.

I have included in the present book the English translation of Śrī Jñāneśvara's 'Prayer for Benediction' which appears in the concluding portion of the Jñāneśvarī, his *magnum opus*, which in my opinion would serve as a fitting epilogue for this book.

I must admit, this is my modest attempt. But I hope the reading of this book may inspire someone to undertake the English translation of the entire Abhaṅgas of Śrī Jñāneśvara which if it ever materialises, would prove to be a great landmark in the literary sphere, since it would benefit the readers unacquainted with Marathi language, by revealing to them the vast treasure of his mystic experiences as reflected in his Abhaṅgas.

I am extremely grateful to Prof. G. W. Kaveeshwar, the celebrated Indian philosopher and an eminent writer and to Dr. Y.M. Pathan, Head, Department of Marathi, Marathwada University, Aurangabad (Maharashtra) and a reputed authority on the works of the Maratha saints, for going through the manuscript of the present work and favouring me with their opinions thereon.

As stated earlier, I have made use of Dr. P.N. Joshi's Marathi book *Śri Jñānadeva Abhaṅga Gāthā* for my present work for which I owe him a deep debt of gratitude. I am also thankful to him for writing a foreword and for making some very valuable suggestions. A short paragraph dealing with 'Virahiṇī form of poetry' has been included in this preface as suggested by Dr. Joshi in his foreword.

P. V. BOBDE

# CONTENTS

## SUBJECTWISE

# A SHORT LIFE-SKETCH
## OF ŚRĪ JÑĀNEŚVARA

Śrī Jñāneśvara, the greatest poet-saint of Mahārāshtra was born at Āḷandī in the year AD 1275. His father's name was Viṭṭhalapanta and mother's Rukmiṇībāī. The family hailed from Āpegāon and was known for piety and great devotion to God. Triṁbakapanta, the great-grandfather of Śrī Jñāneśvara, got his spiritual initiation at the hands of Gorakhanātha of the Nātha sect and his grandfather Govindapanta from Gahinīnātha. Śrī Jñāneśvara's maternal-grandfather Siddheśvara Kulkarṇī was a resident of Āḷandī.

Śrī Jñāneśvara's father Viṭṭhalapanta being of a religious bent of mind from his early age, loved the company of ascetics and became fond of going on pilgrimages. During the course of his wanderings, he happened to visit Āḷāndī. When Sidhopanta Kulkarṇī saw this promising young man, he readily accepted him as his son-in-law. Viṭṭhalapanta and Rukmiṇībāī spent their early days in visiting several sacred places. Viṭṭhalapanta who was a man of spiritual outlook, did not feel at ease in the affairs of the world. He felt a great urge to seek the knowledge of the Brahman, became more and more fond of attending 'Kīrtanas' and felt rejoiced in leading a life of perfect detachment from worldly pleasures and pursuits. The result was, when Viṭṭhalapanta went on a pilgrimage to Kāśī, he got himself initiated as a Sannyāsin by Śrīpāda Svāmī. But when Śrīpāda Svāmī came to know that this initiation did not have the approval of his wife, he bade him go back and resume his erstwhile family life. Even though it was contrary to the popular concept for one to resume the state of married life once having renounced it, Viṭṭhalapanta none the less, adopted it in deference to the behest of his Guru. After resumption of married life with Rukmiṇībāī, four illustrious children—Nivṛtti, Jñāneśvara, Sopāna and Muktābāī—were born to them. Being the children of a 'Sannyāsin', they were treated as outcastes and subjected to severe persecution by the society, but with their hearts full of devotion to God, these children, in the teeth of opposition from the people, continued to lead a life of austerity with their minds fully set on attainment of spiritual knowledge. Efforts were afoot to have the thread-ceremonies of Jñāneśvara and his brothers performed according to Dharma-Śāstra. But the hierarchy of the Brahmin Panditas vehemently opposed the idea and refused to give sanction to their thread-ceremonies as they were the children of a Sannyāsin turned householder. Viṭṭhalapanta could no longer brook the callous treatment meted out to his children and to atone for the 'sin' committed to end his life. The story goes that one day Viṭṭhalapanta and his wife Rukmiṇībāī left their home and went to Allahabad where they renounced their mortal bodies in the holy Gaṅgā.

Now Nivṛttināthа was the mother, father and also the preceptor to these children. They went to Paiṭhaṇa for bringing a writ from the Brahmin Panditas permitting the due performance of their thread-ceremonies. It seems the Brahmins of Paiṭhaṇa must have been greatly impressed by the crystal-like purity of the hearts of these boys and their deep spiritual learning and, therefore, they gave them the required certificate of purification.

Śrī Jñāneśvara, with his brothers, then, came to Nevāse where he wrote his immortal classic *Jñāneśvarī*, a commentary in Marathi on the *Bhagavadgītā*. This was in AD 1290 when he was a lad barely of fifteen years. It is regarded as the best of all the commentaries on the *Bhagavadgītā*. The flight of his fancy, the depth of his spiritual knowledge and the beauty of the figurative language in which he has clothed his exposition, have made *Jñāneśvarī* a great literary work which even today stands unparalleled in Marathi language. Thereafter, Śrī Jñāneśvara wrote his another famous work, *Anubhavāmṛta*, for expounding his own independent reflections on philosophico-religious matters in the light of his spiritual revelations. This work too is regarded as one of the greatest philosophical works in Marathi literature.

Subsequently, Śrī Jñāneśvara accompanied by the famous saint Nāmadeva of Paṇḍharpūra and other saints, went on a pilgrimage to the Northern India. It is in this period that Śrī Jñānadeva is believed to have composed his Abhaṅgas. His Abhaṅgas reveal a very apt and penetrating exposition of spiritual knowledge and devotion Universal fraternity, inherent oneness of all beings and love towards the poor and the downtrodden, are the highlights of his teaching. His exhortation to the people to follow the easy path of devotion eschewing other means of salvation made him a pioneer of the path of devotion—Bhakti Mārga or Bhāgavata Dharma in Mahārāshtra.

Thinking that his life's mission was then fulfilled, Śrī Jñānadeva resolved to bid farewell to this world. Accordingly on the dark thirteenth day of Kārtika in AD 1296, Jñānadeva entered the place of 'Samādhi' at Āḷandī. He sat therein meditating on God and passed away in that state!

# ABHAṄGAS (DEVOTIONAL LYRICS)
## OF ŚRĪ JÑĀNEŚVARA

### 1

O dear! I feel ecstasized when I behold the infatuating form of Śrī Hari.

The selfsame Śrī Viṭṭhala is very handsome. This Mādhava is very pleasing indeed.

I feel deeply attached to Viṭṭhala, only because I have to my credit a heap of righteous deeds from my past lives.

Says Jñāneśvara, the Lord of Rakhumādevī,* our father, is a repository of all happiness. (1)

### 2

A picture of the sun can very well be drawn. But can its splendour be depicted?

One can pretend to be an ascetic, but he may lack the inner spiritual experience.

A man may give sermons on spiritual matters very eloquently, but may find it difficult to tread the path of true renunciation.

Jñāneśvara says, it is only by the grace of his spiritual preceptor that a disciple can have such kind of self-experience. (16)

### 3

O Lord! What shall I call thee?—Saguṇa or Nirguṇa?

When I feel completely bewildered and unable to conclude what the truth is, a sudden awakening dawns on me that thou

---

*Incidentally, it may be stated that the names of Saint Jñāneśvara's father and mother were also the same, viz. Viṭṭhalapanta and Rukmiṇībāī respectively.

God Viṭṭhala is considered as the incarnation of Lord Śrī Kṛṣṇa, the spouse of Rukmiṇī. ('Rakhumāī' is the Prākṛta form of Rukmiṇī).

art the one and the same Govinda in thy Saguṇa form as also in thy Nirguṇa aspect.

No logic can lead me to know thee. Even while exclaiming 'not this, not this!' the Vedas are obliged to point at Govinda only!

What shall I say of thy form?—Is it gross or subtle? Thou art the same Govinda in both the gross and the subtle forms.

Shall I call thee formless or as possessing a form? Thou art the same Govinda in both.

Shall I call thee visible or invisible? Thou art indeed one and the same Govinda in both.

Shall I describe thee as manifest or unmanifest? In both these forms, thou art verily the same Govinda.

Jñāneśvara being blessed by Nivṛttinātha says, this Lord of Rakhumādevī, father Viṭṭhala is alone pervading the entire universe. (18)

4

One who stands at the door of the God's temple even for a moment, with a mind fixed on Him, will have acquired all the four states of salvation. Therefore O people! always repeat the name of Śrī Hari, orally. The vastness of the religious merit acquired by reciting Śrī Hari's name is inestimable.

The performance of the duties of worldly life does not obstruct one's realising Him through uttering His name. Even when you are discharging your duties, let your tongue cultivate the habit of always uttering Śrī Hari's name. The four Vedas and the six Śāstras are exhorting all to follow the only advice of uttering the name of Śrī Hari.

Jñāneśvara says, Śrī Vyāsa has given indications of the significance of uttering Śrī Hari's name in his 'Purāṇas'. Śrī Vyāsa has also elucidated how Śrī Kṛṣṇa, the king of Dvārakā was staying with His devotees, the Pāṇḍavas. (48)

5

A man who receives the knowledge of the self from saints gets rid of his ego and treading on the path of self-realisation attains perfect unity with his divine self.

The camphor when lighted turns instantly into a flame which disappears then and there, the moment the camphor is burnt out. Similarly, a man on attaining self-realisation from the teaching of saints, is freed of all his worldly attachments and desires and in the eyes of the worldly people he becomes a non-entity.

On attaining self-realisation, God's devotee comes nigh salvation. This devotee who has surrendered himself to the saints truly deserves the highest spiritual state he has attained.

Jñāneśvara says, I love to be in the company of such saints. Whether among the people or in the woods, I see Śrī Hari everywhere who is the inner soul of every being. (53)

## 6

And therefore, O human being! as God's name is the sheet anchor of all the philosophies of this world, hold unto it fast in your mind. Only then will Śrī Hari have compassion on you.

It is so very easy to utter the name of 'Rāma-Kṛṣṇa-Govinda'. Now let your tongue start uttering this name without any delay with a fixed mind and yearning heart. There is no other way than this name which you can safely rely upon. Do not therefore follow any other path.

Says Jñāneśvara, observing perfect silence and lodging Śrī Hari in the heart, I have, with a rosary in hand, been ceaselessly uttering his name. (73)

## 7

See! A golden day bathed in the nectar has dawned today, for Śrī Hari whose name I was reciting all the while has manifested himself in my heart!

O Gopāla! Let my mind always think of thee alone. I shall not even for a moment forget Śrī Hari who is the very life-breath of the three worlds.

Jñāneśvara says, O God! I have taken refuge at thy feet and

become one with thee both physically and mentally. I recognise no one except the consort of Rakhumādevī, father Viṭṭhala. (75)

**8**

If an article of camphor is stored in a vessel for a few days, it disappears without leaving any trace whatsoever.

If charcoal is put into the fire, it ceases to exist in the form of a charcoal. Likewise, if we pray to God fixing our mind on Him, we become Jīvanamukta, that is, we attain salvation in this very life.

Jñāneśvara says, the desire for worldly pleasures is indeed illusory and can be overcome by taking recourse to an incessant utterance of the name of Śrī Hari. (91)

**9**

Entertain not a false ego of this mortal body. Instead, why not utter the name 'Viṭṭhala' with your tongue?

Of what avail are these bodily pleasures? For these would come to an abrupt end some day. So better utter the name of Viṭṭhala which is the essence of all the ways of worship.

Says Jñāneśvara, by uttering the name of Rakhumādevī's Lord, father Viṭṭhala, He will surely bless you. Harbour not any doubt whatsoever. (110)

**10**

See! How great the glory of this name is. God Śaṅkara Himself harboured the name of Śrī Rāma in His heart and also advised Pārvatī to do likewise.

The name is thus very nice and is of the highest value. Do give it a place in your heart.

The name of Rāma is more sacred than the water of the Gaṅgā. Even the nectar has proved tasteless before its sweetness.

This name is cooler than sandalwood and more beautiful than gold.

The name is capable of bestowing on you real happiness and salvation and is one that will cut asunder the knots of worldly attachments.

Jñāneśvara says, such an easy and simple name has Rakhumādevī's Lord, father Viṭṭhala provided to his devotees to be uttered by them. (121)

**11**

Yama, the God of Death instructs his messengers: "Listen well to one thing that I say. Do not try to usher into the place where the name of Śrī Rāma is being chanted, as the utterance of this name burns out the greatest of sins, uplifts even a wretch, destroys the sins of this world and is capable of freeing people from the bonds of worldly attachments.

"Do not try to peep into the land where the name of Hari abides, where His devotees utter His name with great faith and where they dance chanting His name with great rejoicing and devotion.

"If you go to snatch people from a place where God Śrī Hari is worshipped with great devotion and where the entire atmosphere is resounding with echoes of the chanting of Hari's name, you yourselves will fall into captivity.

"You should not go to the land where the flags with the symbols of eagles thereon are flying and the banners and buntings are fluttering, for these are the indications that the saints there are deeply engrossed in Hari's love."

Yama further instructs his messengers thus, says Jñāneśvara: "Give heed to one more thing. Where the name of Rāma is being chanted, there Rakhumādevī's Lord, father Viṭṭhala is verily present. Since these devotees of Hari are under His escort, you will not be able to lay your hands on them!" (125)

**12**

Let the line containing the words of Śrī Hari's name be written on your tongue. The words of the name of Kānhā Vanamālī should be clearly written.

The words be so deeply embedded that they would not be effaced afterwards even when your mind is dipped into various worldly passions and pursuits.

The dark-blue and radiant Śrī Hari should remain in my eyes like a pupil.

When the image of Śrī Hari is thus embedded in the tongue and sight, it comes to stabilise even amidst worldly passions.

O Lord Kṛṣṇa! Kindly give a helping hand to enable me to come to thy feet so that this image may remain fixed in my heart.

O Rakhumādevī's Lord, father Viṭṭhala! says Jñāneśvara, if thou remainst in my heart and fillest it from within and without, I shall be enabled to maintain perfect unity with thee. (128)

**13**

As a result of my uttering His name and the company of saints that I am keeping, this Śrī Hari has manifested Himself in my heart filling it with the highest bliss.

I now see Śrī Hari everywhere. Śrī Hari is here. Śrī Hari is there. I do not find any place where He is not.

I long to see Śrī Hari for ever. He alone has filled my mind. I do not see anything else than Śrī Hari.

In my speech I always utter the name of Śrī Hari. Śrī Hari does manifest when I dance chanting His name. A tide of joy begins to fill my heart when I behold Śrī Hari.

This Śrī Hari is at the beginning of the universe. He is at its end also. He is present in all the beings and pervades the entire existence.

Jñāneśvara says, O my people! Make it an endeavour to know this Śrī Hari well. Eulogize Him as best as you can, for this Viṭṭhala, Rakhumādevī's spouse is verily the king of kings! So always remember Him. (133)

**14**

Can sugar be converted into sugar-cane again? Can milk be obtained by churning 'ghī'?

Can a river flow back? Just as these things are impossible, rebirth for the devotees of God is also an impossibility.

Those who spend their lives in the service of God in manifold ways will never fall again into the snare of worldly pursuits. Can anyone write with the ink of camphor? Can we touch our shadow at the very sunrise?

Can the lame run after the wind? As these are utter improbabilities, so also God's devotees will not get re-birth. Those who speak ill of saints and the devotees of Śrī Hari are indeed slaves of worldly passions.

Says Jñāneśvara, those who sing the praise of God with their hearts full of earnest devotion are relieved of the cycle of rebirth. This I, the disciple of Nivṛttinātha, say unto you on oath. (177)

## 15

In my previous life, I had done enormous deeds of merit which are thus now bearing fruit in this life.

Today, I am very happy to have met these saints. On seeing them I no longer desire even to meet my parents, brothers or relatives and friends!

These saints are more venerable than even the well-known places of pilgrimage. Lord Śyāmasundara stands out pre-eminent amidst their congregation.

How does one feel on meeting them? The feeling which a man on meeting them experiences can be compared to a pauper's when he comes to possess a big treasure or to the feeling of a lifeless being, returning to life.

I feel the same kind of joy on meeting the saints which a separated calf feels when it meets its mother or a young deer gone astray feels when it beholds its mother.

The joy I feel on meeting the saints far outweighs the pleasure I might get from tasting the nectar! I had today the fortune to meet such devotees of the Lord of Paṇḍharapūra.

Says Jñāneśvara, by the grace of Rakhumādevī's Lord, father Viṭṭhala, I had a chance to meet these saints and my worldly cares and sorrows have thereby vanished altogether. (190)

## 16

By Śrī Hari's grace, I shall spread the gospel of devotion (Bhakti) and strive to alleviate the sufferings of the poor and the distressed. Thus I shall fill all the three worlds with divine joy. This is my vow.

For the purpose of getting the blessings of Lord Pāṇḍuraṅga, I shall go to Paṇḍharapūra even as a married young lady visits her parental home and shall see Him who is both father and mother to me.

In this visit, I shall embrace Lord Pāṇḍuraṅga and shall secure from Him the fruit of my meritorious deeds.

Says Jñāneśvara, when I met Rakhumādevī's consort, father Viṭṭhala, so much was He pleased that He treated me as His bosom-friend! (221)

## 17

O Śrī Kṛṣṇa! The light of millions of moons is shining on your forehead. O Lotus-eyed, Smiling-faced Śrī Kṛṣṇa! Please favour us with thy divine smile at least once.

O Śrī Kṛṣṇa! Please move for us, nod for us. Also have frequent chats with us.

Says Jñāneśvara, see how this Rakhumādevī's Lord, father Viṭṭhala, acceding to our request, is moving His hand! (242)

## 18

O Gopāla! awake. Open thine charming and enchanting eyes. The night of ignorance is over and the rays of the sun of knowledge have spread everywhere. The cattle in the form of senses are leaving for the woods of Nirguṇa. The turbulent calves of the refracting mind have become unruly whom thou alone canst control.

The night of three-fold guṇas has ended and the dawn of awakening has ushered in. The radiant day-break in the form of Śrī Guru's grace has appeared.

The sun of self-realisation will immediately follow and the moon with its satellites representing bodily attachment will then fade away of itself.

The delusion that the stars are still visible in the sky will also disappear forthwith. The Ātman in the form of the dark-blue bee incarcerated in the lotus will then be liberated.

Intellect and knowledge in the form of the 'Cakravāka' pair will soon be reunited and the night lotus of attachment towards bodily pleasures shall wither away.

Flames of non-attachment, arising out of the sun of knowledge of the All-conscious divine Self when manifest, will burn away all the woods of sensual desires.

The wild beasts of diverse external pleasures will suffer extinction in the wake of the unique deluge, for the mirage of worldly passions will deceive none but fools.

See! The gatherings of ascetics have, in these early hours of the mornings, started treading on the path of the knowledge of 'yoga' and the cuckoos with their chirp are expressing the meaning of the Upaniṣads!

Those who had indulged in futile polemics like owls have retreated to their abodes and have become speechless. All the polemics about the mandates of the four Vedas and six Śāstras have come to a close. A seeker after self-realisation has got rid of his frailties and has forsaken the desire for worldly pleasures.

Jñāneśvara says, by the grace of Śrī Nivṛttinātha, a seeker for salvation attains the status of a 'yogī' and experiences a divine bliss in the early hours of such a pleasant morning. (246)

**19**

A crow has started cawing on the yonder side of the house since long and it seems it is suggesting a good omen of the arrival of a guest.

O crow! You who are portending an omen, please fly away. Do fly away. I shall adorn your feet with gold. But tell me only this much when the Lord of Paṇḍharī is coming to my house as a guest.

O crow! I shall fill your beak with curds and rice, but tell me quickly when Paṇḍharīnātha, who is so dear to my heart will meet me.

I shall offer you a pot-ful of milk but tell me with certainty when this Viṭṭhala is coming to my house.

O crow! You may even taste the sweet mangoes which are on the branch of the tree standing by my door, but tell me some good news of a presage to happen today. Says Jñāneśvara, O crow! please disclose to me some sign of an omen indicating that Lord Paṇḍharīnātha will meet me early! (276)

**20**

Since I am all the while meditating on the dark-blue Lord, I perceive the entire sky as blue. The love for Śrī Kṛṣṇa is blue. The entire universe seems to be evenly manifested in blue.

The Brahman is blue, 'karma' is blue, all 'Āśrama' routine is blue and my Śrī Gurunātha also appears to be blue!

All daily acts, partaking of food and whatever I see are all done with a mind filled with this bluish hue.

Says Jñāneśvara, in becoming one with the dark-blue Paramātman I have also been rapt up in blueness; Aye, truly lost! (327)

**21**

I have planted in my courtyard the wish-yielding tree of 'Cintāmaṇi' and have fed it with the lustrous water of the pearls of my devotion through the bluish channels.

In truth, we are deeply engrossed in this worldly life under the influence of illusion but have been saved by our close association with Lord Kṛṣṇa.

Lord Śrī Kṛṣṇa—a radiant gem available in a quarry of diamonds—is found by me in my own courtyard!

The sun, the moon and their rays have all emanated from Him.

My joy knows no bounds when I see the Lord in the form of the 'wish-tree' and the 'wish-jewel'.

Just as the creepers present a bright and vigorous look and become laden with flowers and fruits after receiving heavy showers of rain preceded by thunder, even so, says Jñāneśvara, my heart leapt with ecstacy when I beheld Lord Śrī Kṛṣṇa! (329)

## 22

The cool and pleasant light of the moon and the radiance of the sun are lost in the divine splendour of the Lord.

The Lord who is the very life of the three worlds, is the cause of this universe which is as minute as an atom.

Jñāneśvara says, this consort of Rakhumādevī, father Viṭṭhala is both Saguṇa and Nirguṇa and I have had an experience that He is subtle as an atom! (339)

## 23

How has this Nirguṇa Paramātman shown Himself at my door? He has no root, that is, beginning, neither branches nor offshoots! Strangely enough, He appears in His stately Saguṇa form even though He is Nirguṇa and displays His unique magnificence in the souls of living beings and as an universal soul too.

The ways of His pervasiveness and His sport are beyond comprehension. By His sweet will, He manifests Himself in the form of the universe, only for the sake of His own pleasure.

Says Jñāneśvara, no one can comprehend His greatness even though He is present in all the animate and inanimate things in the universe. (340)

## 24

Believing that thou art distinct from me, I tried to see thee, but experienced that my body, mind as also the entire universe are all filled by thee alone!

What a wonder! The whole world is found permeated with Śrī Hari. Therefore, there now remains nothing like my remembering thee or forgetting thee. Both have become meaningless. What can I do?

Says Jñāneśvara, see what this Lord of Rakhumādevī, Śrī Viṭṭhala has done! Just as iron is changed into gold by a touch of the philosophers' stone, likewise, everything appeared to have been filled with Viṭṭhala, the moment I realised Him! (352)

**25**

This Viṭṭhala has subdued my mind and freed me from the ties of the world and has fully weeded out my sense of I-ness.

Abiding in my eyes, He has enchanted me.

Jñāneśvara says, this Viṭṭhala is very alluring. Giving me shelter in His form, He has made me happy. (354)

**26**

I long to merge altogether in thy form, to keep thee in my heart and to behold thy real form which is in fact formless!

I yearn to disclose to thee all the secrets of my heart and with lips sealed, to converse with thee in silence!

Jñāneśvara says, I have made entreaties to this Lord of Rakhumādevī who having been pleased with me, revealed me His divine form—the Brahman. (363)

**27***

O Lord! Thou callest thyself our parents and even then tormentest us by binding us to the (cycle of) births (and deaths)! Thou tellest that thou hast created this entire universe and art its prop. But I fail to experience the concept which tells that 'wherever there is life, there God is!'

A caterpillar by brooding (over a black-bee) is transformed into a black-bee. Why can we not likewise attain Śiva-hood—salvation?

Thou imposest on us a heavy punishment even for a trivial mistake. What are the hymns or other remedial prescriptions open

*From the fifth stanza onwards.

to us for getting rid of our defects? In what manner are we to remove these blemishes? On giving a thought to thy form, we find that it is indestructible. But here our bodies have been torn asunder and devoured by all-devouring Death in thy very presence, even though we happen to be thy children! Why canst thou not take pity on us? Why art thou putting us to grief by subjecting us to frequent rebirths?

Truly speaking, we see in the mirror only our own image. It is none else's. When the sun rises, we see its rays which disappear when it sets. Likewise, the enlightenment, "I am He", dawns on a person out of the discourse of his spiritual preceptor and he comes to experience the unity of his self with the Supreme Spirit. If the truth is something else, then kindly advise me accordingly. How often shall I go on requesting you?

Nothing escapes the clutches of Death. For meditating, therefore, on the Supreme Brahman, the ascetics retire to woods. Of these, some roam naked, some wear saffron robes, some pluck out their hair with hands, some take to renunciation out of the fear of death, some go to a forest to practise 'Prāṇāyāma' for contemplating on the Supreme Spirit and some subdue their senses for controlling their sensual desires. But even after resorting to all these practices, they hardly stand to get any experience of bliss.

Does not a ripple appearing on the surface of water merge in the water itself? Likewise, O the Giver! We are as waves in thy form. How has then this attachment to worldly life developed? Why should then there arise such a wide gap between thou, the great Lord, and we, the insignificant persons? To me it appears, the whole thing is deceptive! Why not tell us what the truth is?

When salt falls into water or water falls over salt they become one. How could they retain their separateness in attributes? Iron is changed into gold by a touch of the Philosophers' stone!

O Rakhumādevī's Lord, father Viṭṭhala! Do not now put me to rebirth again. Swearing in thy name, I pray this to thee earnestly. (392)

## 28*

An ignorant person rejoices in pursuing external pleasures just as a dog chews a piece of an old bone in the saliva of its mouth with great satisfaction!

An assemblage of hands and feet of persons is a body, but they love it so dearly. This is indeed repulsive.

Parents are only a nominal cause of their progeny. Truly speaking, a child is born according to its destiny. Under a misconception, however, it feels pleasure in resting in the lap of its parents. But it is like taking shelter in its own false shadow!

Parents take care of their children. They also provide them protection. With fond love they satisfy the desires of their senses too. But whom to regard as the real master is the most significant question in this world.

For a deer to pursue incessantly the mirage as it advances, is nothing else but a futile exercise. A human being is likewise deluded.

Says Jñāneśvara, O Lord! How much shall I tell thee about this worldly life? Thou are the sole monarch of this universe. Once we come to realise thee, how could the worldly dreams of an unending cycle of births and deaths last for long? (393)

## 29*

O the Munificent! Now my eyes shall have a full view of thee. I shall embrace thee from all sides. With my mouth, I shall speak with thee alone. With my feet, I shall walk down to see thee only.

Thus shall I spend the whole of my time for thee alone. So much I am enchanted with thy devotion that I have no liking left for anything else.

We see our reflection in the mirror, but the moment the mirror is withdrawn, the reflection disappears uniting with the seer! Similarly, I have unexpectedly been attached to thy form which is

*From Fifth stanza onwards.

*From Fourth stanza onwards.

present in the beginning, in the middle and in the end of this cosmos, and have now merged in it.

Now that I see nothing else but thee, the duality has disappeared. When I do not see thee as a separate entity, how can the egoistic 'I' ever exist? And how absurd it is to say that the unity has taken place when, in fact, it existed from the very beginning!

Jñāneśvara says, thus even though Śrī Hari might be very close to a man, but so long as he has not attained His knowledge, he will remain spiritually hungry. Truly speaking, the talk of one's feeling satisfied or otherwise is altogether meaningless, once the realisation of God is achieved. As for myself, I have attained oneness with Rakhumādevī's Lord, father Viṭṭhala. (398)

## 30

The moon presents a very beautiful appearance on the full-moon day, but at 'Amāvasyā' when its digits disappear altogether, it is completely divested of its brilliance.

Similarly, O Lord! When all the beings owe their beauty to thee, why art thou so unkind to have made them mortal?

If the camphor forsakes its sweet scent, what is it that others would stand to lose?

The waves on the surface of water in the ocean take refuge into the ocean only. They have no other support.

Limbs, head and the body are in fact all one. Likewise, to serve thee is to become one with thee.

Jñāneśvara says, O the Lord of Rakhumādevī, King of Kings! I did not intend to talk, but have spoken with a view only to enhance the dignity of thy devotion. (400)

## 31

Who has dispelled the darkness of ignorance from my mind? Before whose radiance has the sun's splendour grown pale? O enchanting Śrī Kṛṣṇa! Thou alone hast done it! Is not Lord Śrī Kṛṣṇa like a full moon appearing after the period of dark nights to make the bird 'cakora' feed on the nectarine juice drizzling from its rays and to blossom the night-blooming lotus? To talk about thy from is so very mysterious indeed!

We are the thirsty 'cakora' birds and thou art verily the moon who quenches our thirst! We are completely satisfied by tasting the nectar of thy name. Of all the wise, thou art the wisest and the life of all lives! Thou art the dearest kin who provides thy devotees with a treasure of thy love! The four Vedas and the six Śāstras attempt to describe thy form. But they only agree to disagree! Such is thy queer versatility. O the Munificent Viṭṭhala! Whom and how are we to blame?

I am fascinated by thy name and my tongue feels pleasure in uttering it. I rejoice in singing thy unfathomable fame and glory. May, therefore, my mind always remain filled with thy love, for it is thou who art alone present in the inner self of all beings.

Thou dost disavow all those who are disposed to dry polemics. The 'Śrutis', for this reason, could not dive deeper and discontinuing all efforts to describe thee could only say 'not this, not this'! Thou art really Nirguṇa but I saw thee in thy Saguṇa form! O the Bountiful one! I do not at all comprehend who thou really art. I, therefore, entreat thee not to act in a way as would increase my perplexity further. Please foster love for thee in my heart that I may see thy vision in the Saguṇa form.

Says Jñāneśvara, we should, therefore, make an endeavour to see Him in Saguṇa form instead of trying to concentrate our mind on His Nirguṇa form. Why should anyone pursue futilely to see Him in His Nirguṇa form? O the Giver! Who is capable of seeing thy form which not only is filled in all the ten senses of the body like ten highways of a city, but pervades the entire universe?

O Rakhumādevī's Lord, father Viṭṭhala! We should see thy Saguṇa form to our hearts' content. To me this appears to be an easier path leading to salvation. (403)

## 32

O Lord Śrī Kṛṣṇa! On hearing all thy virtues and glory, the eagerness of my mind has risen to a high pitch and I have become impatient to embrace thee.

My body, mind and tongue having been completely lost in thy contemplation, I have ceased to see myself as a separate entity. I have forgotten myself altogether!

I have with an impatient mind lifted my arms to embrace thee, but alas! I was deluded as I had no clear comprehension of thy form.

Jñāneśvara says, my gazing at thy face has also ceased. This Rakhumādevī's spouse, father Viṭṭhala has reduced me to this state! (406)

## 33

Has seed emerged from the fruit or the fruit from the seed ? It is, indeed, very difficult to say. That is why it is impossible to trace out the origin of a leaf or of a flower.

O God! I do not likewise understand the intricacies of the stupendous structure of this universe. Nor can I comprehend any of the theories underlying the creation of this universe.

Is the earth formed of dust or the dust formed from the earth? This question too baffles solution.

Says Jñāneśvara, this Rakhumādevī's Lord, father Viṭṭhala has filled the entire universe incessantly from within and without! (408)

## 34

As the gross body is perishable, it is sure to go under the earth some day. I shall feel highly gratified when Śrī Hari would tread over the place under which my body would lie buried!

Whether my body is alive or dead, it is my earnest desire to have an undying faith in Lord Pāṇḍuraṅga.

The second element in the body is water. I shall exist in the form of water of the Gaṅgā and bathe the Lord day and night. I shall thus sport on the body of the Lord.

Splendour is the third element. I shall become a big lamp and adorn the row of lights in the courtyard of Śrī Hari's temple.

The fourth element is air. By becoming a fan, I shall please

Śrī Hari by bringing to Him cool refreshing breezes. That is my firm resolve.

The fifth element is space in which form I shall stay in His stately mansion.

Says Jñāneśvara, O Rakhumādevī's Lord, father Viṭṭhala! Let my mind always dwell on thee. Let it not swerve at any time from this resolve. (409)

## 35

I neither seek worldly pleasures nor salvation. I shall not put thee in a predicament on my account because thou and I have been intimately associated with each other from the very beginning. A life is always marked by vicissitudes. If some untoward acts have been committed by me without knowing thee, thou shalt surely ponder over it. O the Giver! even then I would not speak plainly before thee.

There appear numerous ripples on the surface of water which finally merge with it. Who is able to separate them?

The earth takes different shapes according to different moulds it is put into. Similarly, all the beings with their manifold forms contain the selfsame Paramātman! O the Giver! there is thus no difference between my 'Self' and thy Supreme Self.

O the cowherd Śrī Kṛṣṇa! It is because of the limiting condition, viz. the mirror that a man sees in it his reflection which lasts till the mirror is there. Can therefore the disc and its reflection be considered as different? Even if several ornaments of gold are made, the gold in them is the same. Likewise, there is practically little difference between I the individual soul and thou the Universal Soul. The difference, if any, is only in names.

The gust howsoever great, ultimately merges with the sky. There is a natural unity between us in the same way.

Says Jñāneśvara, O the Munificent one! Is the space within a pot different from that in the sky itself? O the Paramount Lord! Thou and I are likewise really one. Rakhumādevī's Lord, father Viṭṭhala is the only one who is the enjoyer of this world. The talk that the world is different from Him is all futile. (410)

36

I should see only thee with my eyes. My ears should hear only thy praise.

I should meditate only on thy form and my feet should walk only towards thee.

Says Jñāneśvara, Śrī Nivṛttinātha has filled my heart with Rakhumādevī's Lord, father Viṭṭhala to the brim. (414)

37

O Lord! I have been playing the game of this worldly life relying solely on thy support. In this game, therefore, thou shouldst always be with me.

Thou plungest me in the battle of this worldly life, but thou dost not feel any compassion for me.

I have stepped into the battlefield of this worldly life with great courage. But, here, I do not find any trace of anything.

Jñāneśvara says, if we reverse our attitude for external pleasures and turn it inwards to God through meditation the state of salvation is reached and the cycle of births and deaths comes to a stop. (419)

38

See, how small the piece of cloth of a king's flag is. But the king has to fight so many odds to protect it. Likewise, O Lord! even though my authority in the spiritual sphere might be as insignificant as that rag of cloth, it nonetheless bears the imprint of thy seal!

How small is a deed of gift made by a king? But the king's authority enhances its significance!

Says Jñāneśvara, O thou, the Lord of Rakhumādevī, father Viṭṭhala! Mayst thou kindly keep thy vow as a saviour of thy devotees. (420)

39

O my soul! By always talking of " 'I', mine and my family,"

you are carrying on the activities of this body in the world in vain. Instead, O Lord! create in my mind a feeling that the things of the world do not belong to me but stand dedicated to the very places from which they originated, and thus enable me to secure a complete detachment from this worldly life.

The sensual pleasures keep on alluring you the more you run after them but prove disastrous in the end. It is, therefore, better to have no truck with them.

O Lord! While creating this human body, thou, puttest in it the weights of the three 'guṇas'—Sattva, Rajas and Tamas—and hurlest us in the deluge of this worldly life. The life is then caught up in the whirlpool. How is it going to be saved from this peril?

O Lord! How long should I continue to describe to thee the woeful tale of this delusive mundane life? Thou, thereby, dost not seem to feel any compassion for me. Says Jñāneśvara, O Rakhumādevī's Lord, father Viṭṭhala! my mind has been yearning ceaselessly to merge in thee. (421)

**40**

O Śrī Kṛṣṇa! I am stranded in a distant land far away from thee. I cannot now bear the pangs of thy separation which have subjected me to a severe mental anguish.

The night appears to me as day. Enticing me thus thou hast forsaken me. Why dost thou not come back?

Says Jñāneśvara, O Rider of the Eagle, the Sedate, the Munificent, Rakhumādevī's Lord, father Viṭṭhala! I beseech thee to meet me as early as possible. (423)

**41**

If God wills, what is it that will not happen? Even a stone boat will float on water!

A row of ants could tread on the rope of sun-beams and crops could grow even on a volcanic plateau (or fiery surface).

Legs could shoot forth to inanimate walls and they could

begin to walk. A mosquito could equal Merū, the highest among mountains!

Says Jñāneśvara, even the unprecedented act of realisation of the Supreme Spirit could be accomplished by the grace of Śrī Guru Nivṛttinātha. (425)

**42**

The form of God is captivating! Have, therefore, a constant look at it. By steadfastly gazing at it, your identity will completely merge with it!

Know that you are no other than Śrī Hari! You will not then be required to take recourse to other means for realising Him.

Says Jñāneśvara, the darkness of ignorance having no real existence disappears without the appearance of the sun's disk. This fundamental truth I have come to know by the grace of Śrī Nivṛtti. (471)

**43**

As all the holy places lie at the feet of Śrī Nivṛttinātha, O my mind, have a dip in them.

By the grace of my spiritual preceptor, my heart is cleansed and I shall not wander in the delusion of the body being the soul.

Just as a wave in the ocean ceases to exist when it merges in the ocean, even so I have become one with the Supreme Brahman.

Jñāneśvara says, see what a miracle has been wrought by Rakhumādevī's consort, Śrī Viṭṭhala! A boat has been lost in the mirage! How wonderful! My bodily existence being nothing else but an illusion only, has therefore, automatically merged with the Universal Spirit. (472)

**44**

Says Nivṛttinātha, in this universe which has taken shape,

the gross sight is unable to see the Paramātman. Endeavour should therefore be made to seek the formless Paramātman.

When the illusion from which has originated the form, has itself merged with the Paramātman, what is it that would survive? A number of Śāstras, therefore, advise you to realise the Paramātman by constantly meditating on Him.

O my gracious Guru! I beseech you to enlighten me of what the void is born of and what survives after it disappears.

Thereupon Śrī Guru says, 'I shall first explain you what the words 'form' and 'formless' mean to enable you to decide whether God has a form or is devoid of it. Truly speaking, the talk of 'form' or 'formlessness' is all futile. Better see within yourself the Paramātman without worrying about His form.

'However, by simply knowing this, you may not be able to experience it. But to realise your Ātman is the only experience to be sought after. Strive, therefore, to stay in this experience.

Where is the day or where is the night where the sun and the moon merge in the form of the Paramātman? They are real masters of Yoga who get such an experience.

In such a state, action and inaction disappear and religion and worship lose their significance!

The relation between a preceptor and his disciple too disappears and all experience as such merges into the sea of the Paramātman!

Such a state is to be experienced just like enjoying the sweetness of sugar without tasting! There you have to speak without tongue and to see without eyes! This state is known as the 'Brahman'.

One who steps out in the dark taking a lamp in hand in search of darkness, will not find any darkness but light only.

Jñāneśvara says, in the same way, Rakhumādevī's Lord, father Viṭṭhala is the Seer and because of His nature as Knowledge Absolute the duality between the vision and the visionariness comes to an end! (478)

**45**

My misconception of the body being the soul having died down what is it that I should see and where should I see and what is it that I should partake of on feeling hungry?

Where the act of seeing itself has ceased, what is that to be seen? If the object for concentration itself does not exist, what is that which the mind should fix itself upon?

How should a picture be drawn if there is no wall? And which is the place where it is to be kept on completion?

Says Jñāneśvara, meditate on this Rakhumādevī's Lord, father Viṭṭhala and then see what happens. (486)

## 46

The Brahman which is neither near nor far in the expanse of this colossal universe dwells at the bottom of the mind.

This Brahman is not discernible in the light of the sun, but is verily present even in a mosquito!

It can neither be truly described in words nor perceived by physical sight.

Like devouring a gross body without teeth or destroying a subtle body without weapons, this eternal Brahman has wrought a miracle. While I was treading on the path of self-realisation as shown by Śrī Nivṛttinātha, it dispelled my sense of dualism and disappeared after revealing to me the unity existing between me and the Supreme Spirit.

Says Jñāneśvara, O Jñāneśvara, disciple of Śrī Nivṛttinātha! concentrate on Rakhumādevī's Lord, father Viṭṭhala instead of indulging in too much talk. (494)

## 47

He who acquires true knowledge by the grace of his spiritual preceptor alone will attain the Supreme Brahman. He will realise that the All-pervading is present in the Supreme Spirit.

When I saw the Paramātman pervading everywhere, it was His formless state that I witnessed. On seeing Him thus, I felt gratified.

If a doll of camphor is brought in contact with the flame of camphor, they become one. Likewise, I have been united with Him.

Says Jñāneśvara, this Paramātman has neither any form nor shadow or semblance. He transcends the three Guṇas and also Māyā. To think thus is the only way to realise Rakhumādevī's consort, father Viṭṭhala. (511)

48

The form of Paramātman cannot be conceived by any means. He cannot be described by drawing any number of inferences. This Śrī Hari who is thus inconceivable and ineffable have I ultimately realised by my singular devotion.

I attained a stage almost close to salvation and gradually came to be blessed by the formless Paramātman.

In this state, a strange thing has happened. In describing the experience of His grace, speech becomes dumb! Such glorious Paramātman, Rakhumādevī's Lord, father Viṭṭhala have I realised by my persistent efforts. (514)

49

Śrī Hari is present evenly at the beginning, in the middle and at the end of this world. He is present in a pitcher as also in a monastery!

Such invisible Paramātman have I seen while meditating on Him. When I saw Him pervading everywhere like air, I could secure mental peace and equanimity.

Since I was firmly devoted to the omniscient Paramātman, I could forsake my worldly pursuits and lead a life of perfect detachment due to his association.

Says Jñāneśvara, where there is always love for Hari's name, there alone lies His resting place. (535)

50

I have filled the pot of my heart which is as clean and pure as a camphor, with the juice of my experience of being the Brahman (itself). As a result, the nose with the sweet scent has dissolved in it!

Truly speaking, it has no taste, no scent, no joy, no grief nor anything whatsoever.

Says Jñāneśvara, my mind lies fully attached to the spouse of Rakhumādevi, father Viṭṭhala and now nothing is left with me. The essence of the teaching of the four Vedas is also the same. (554)

**51**

Just as a 'Cātaka' bird concentrates its mind all the while on a cloud, in the same way, my mind always remains fixed on the Paramātman abiding in the innermost recesses of my heart and the cloud of Brahman pours down on me showers of the nectar of Lord Śrī Kṛṣṇa's grace.

As this nectar has become the fountain-spring of my life, there is now nothing else left to sustain me.

Says Jñāneśvara, I have touched this Rakhumādevi's spouse, father Viṭṭhala without my hands and seen Him—my Brahman —without my eyes! (563)

**52**

The Paramātman is Nirguṇa when we consider Him as Saguṇa, and Saguṇa when we think of Him to be Nirguṇa. In fact, there is no difference between the two.

Just as gold contains ornaments and ornaments are comprised of gold, or just as a house is built of mud and is reduced to mud ultimately, even so Nirguṇa exists in the Saguṇa, and Saguṇa in the Nirguṇa. It is only the attributes of things which make them either small or great. But the Saguṇa or Nirguṇa God by whatever epithet He may be termed, is basically one and the same.

Says Jñāneśvara, this world, as also the other world, the body and the entire universe are all incessantly filled with Brahman. (585)

**53**

While looking at God, I lost the very consciousness that I was looking at Him! O God! I felt extremely happy because of the supreme bliss that I experienced!

Now, that I am myself filling the whole world, what sense is there in seeing my own form?

I do not witness any other thing whatsoever in this universe. All the fourteen worlds seems to be filled with Brahman alone. O God! this I say swearing in thy name.

There remains no duality now between us. The very consciousness of my self has foresaken me.

Says Jñāneśvara, I have realised Him, who alone is pervading the entire universe. I have become merged in Him. (587)

## 54

Where there is joy, there is sorrow, and sorrow where there is joy. Similarly there is unity in diversity and diversity in unity!

Where there is God, there is His devotee and where there is devotee, there is God. There is no divergence between the two.

Where there is shadow, there is a tree, and a tree, where there is shadow. Likewise, where there is a disciple there is his Guru, and where there is a Guru, there is bound to be his disciple.

A particle means the earth and the earth means a particle. Similarly, where there is illusion, there are attributes, and where there are attributes, there is illusion.

Jñāneśvara says, by the grace of my spiritual preceptor, I have had realisation that it is I who am pervading the entire world. I could know this secret by the grace of Nivṛttī. (608)

## 55

The flame shining forth in the bud of the heart has united with Brahman.

Just as salt assimilates with water of the sea, the mind has united with Brahman.

Just as a tree is contained in its seed, or a drop of water is absorbed in the earth, similarly, the self has become one with the Supreme Spirit. Words have merged in the speechless being of the Paramātman!

Says Jñāneśvara, since there is thus non-duality in the entire universe, how can there exist a notion of separate identities of 'I' and 'you'? I have really become the Brahman itself. (610)

## 56

Rivers may flow in a reverse direction and climb on a high mountain like Brahmagiri, but a person who has attained the knowledge of the Supreme Spirit, can have no rebirth.

A sandal tree could even be transformed into an acacia tree, but a man of spiritual wisdom will not be reborn.

A burnt camphor may again revert to its original form, but a man of enlightenment will not be born again.

Wind may even be caught in a net but a learned man will get no rebirth.

Jñāneśvara says, since I have attained spiritual knowledge, I am freed from the cycle of births and deaths! (613)

## 57

Just as foodgrains cannot be grown on a volcanic plateau, even so, men having attained the knowledge of Brahman are not affected by the joys and sorrows of life.

Just as a void is not discernible in the dark, so also, a man of wisdom gets rid of the Māyā (illusion).

Just as the brightness of the moon cannot be diminished by the light of the stars, even so a man of spiritual wisdom is not affected by good end evil.

Says Jñāneśvara, O Rakhumādevi's spouse Viṭhoba! such an enlightened person having been freed from the net of illusion, remains unaffected by good and evil. (614)

## 58

All the living beings in this world are born of Rajas constituent. Sattva sustains them and Tamas destroys them. Such is the nature of this world which comprises of the three Guṇas or properties.

Forsaking the three Guṇas we should acquire a state which is beyond them. For this, we should rise above good and bad conduct.

Says Jñāneśvara, if this is accomplished, only then you would receive the grace of your spiritual preceptor and would come to experience the bliss of salvation in this very life. (621)

**59**

Just as a tortoise draws in its limbs, in the same way, the Ātman, residing in the body illumines the senses.

Like a lamp shining of itself, this embodied Ātman manifests itself through the limbs!

Truly speaking, this Ātman is never born nor dies. Know that He is only a witness to all the activities of life.

Life is an illusory form of the Ātman and mind an outcome of ignorance. That is why a human being falls into the snare of the worldly life.

Says Jñāneśvara, the Ātman, being perfectly pure and enlightened, is free from all bondages. (624)

**60**

The Brahman is more pervasive than the sky, sets in motion even the wind and is more effulgent than fire.

Brahman is eternal, all-pervasive, without a beginning and is a cloud full of joy.

Jñāneśvara says, the Brahman transcends all things visible and I feel that I have no different identity than that of my Guru who is the incarnation of the Supreme Spirit. (627)

**61**

Rivers overflow in rainy season and meet the sea.

When the summer returns, they become dry, but the sea, thereby, is not affected.

Likewise, the ascetics and the men of virtue when visited by happiness or sufferings falling to their lot according to their past deeds, do not feel perturbed but maintain perfect equanimity.

They experience that the same Brahman exists in all the beings.

The teaching that 'You are Brahman!' being embedded in their minds, they do not, at all, feel that this world, which they witness, has any separate existence.

True knowledge dawns on them dispelling their ignorance. The result is, their minds are purged of perverseness and become purified.

Says Jñāneśvara, whether water flows or is stagnant, it is nonetheless water. Likewise, I have merged in the Brahman. (633)

**62**

Howsoever beautifully constructed a house might be, if there is no light in it, it loses all its charm.

Just as a meal without 'Ghī', a mouth (after meals) without a 'Tāmbula', a throat without music are all charmless, even so a learned man is of little significance if he has no spiritual experience.

A woman may be quite young and beautiful, but if she is without a husband, her fascination has no meaning.

A man of riches who eschews giving gifts, or an orator not having any listeners are of little significance. Similar is the case of an erudite person who does not know the Vedas.

Says Jñāneśvara, it does little credit to a man who indulges in a rhetorical talk on the knowledge of Brahman, but lacks spiritual experience. (636)

**63**

Why are you so much worried about your body which, in fact, is nothing else but earth? Instead, why not try to know who you are?

Why do you attach so much importance to your worldly life? Why bear its burden?

You are verily a pure, enlightened and complete entity and are beyond birth and death.

You are under a misconception because of your sheer ignorance. Therefore, with the knowledge obtained from your spiritual preceptor, cut asunder the knot of this worldly life.

Jñāneśvara says, with the grace of Śrī Guru, you shall certainly cross over the ocean of this worldly life. (638)

**64**

Why are you running hither and thither searching God? Why not recognise God who abides in your own heart?

In truth, God has neither a form nor a name. He has no special abode either.

Says Jñāneśvara, worship therefore, that God who is with you in the form of your Ātman and serve Him ceaselessly. (647)

**65**

Yoga is very difficult of achievement. Even after making strenuous efforts, you are not able to master it. And so you fail to realise God. I am, therefore, telling you the secret of my heart.

It is not necessary for you either to control the mind or to subdue the senses. Instead only do this: wheresoever your mind goes astray, imagine your Sadguru's feet to be there. Knowledge of Brahman will then dawn on you.

Jñāneśvara says, endeavour to become Nirguṇa, and you will come to know fully the secret of the knowledge of Self. (649)

**66**

O brother! why do you harbour so much vanity about yourself? Better realise that all human beings are equal. Know that the universal Atman vibrates through all beings.

The Ātman is present alike in the smallest atom, in the grass, in the wood, in the stones and in all other things.

If there is any disparity or inequality, it is of the body only. The Ātman is present equally in all the beings. But the ignorant erroneously lay the blame at the door of the Ātman.

Says Jñāneśvara, he should be called a perfect Yogī who sees not diversity but unity only amongst all beings. (651)

## 67

To put some 'Kusumbā' in milk when it is being heated in a golden pot and thus to spoil it!

To cut down sandal and plantain trees and in their stead to plant acacia trees and to guard them!

To cultivate the land carefully and sow in it seeds of the poisonous plant of the white thorn-apple!

All these are nothing but futile exercises.

Says Jñāneśvara, instead of indulging in such pranks, you should surrender to your spiritual preceptor with a devoted mind. (652)

## 68

When a caterpillar meditates continuously on the dark-blue bee, its metamorphosis takes place and it become the bee itself. It ceases to be the insect as it originally existed. Similarly, if you constantly meditate on the Brahman, the knots of your worldly life are cut asunder and your self merges into the Brahman.

Once the impurities are removed from gold, what remains is but pure gold. The same is the case with the eternal Brahman. The relation between the Self and the Supreme Self is primeval but due to the attributes of Māyā, men succumb to delusion.

Says Jñāneśvara, he is a true Yogī who after careful thought realises that all the beings are truly one. (654)

## 69

I planted a seedling of the knowledge of the self by my door which grew into a mighty creeper spreading over the entire sky!

This Mogarā creeper then yielded beautiful flowers of the 'Ātman-principle' in so much exuberance that by the time their sweet scent was being enjoyed numerous other buds started blooming!

Says Jñāneśvara, in my fancy, I wove them into a beautiful garland and offered it to the lord of Rakhumādevi, father Viṭṭhala. (663)

## 70

When we have a protector like Śrī Gurunātha, why should we go on counting the treasures of others? Does the wife of a king go on begging alms? She gets at her bidding whatever is desired by her. What is it that a person sitting under the wish-yielding tree would ever lack?

Says Jñāneśvara, I have been saved by the grace of Śrī Guru. I have been uplifted. (676)

## 71

Resting on a cosy bed of equanimity I am fulfilling my mission with the grace of Śrī Nivṛttinātha.

The earth is my bed and the sky a covering for my body.

Compassion towards all beings is the very essence of life. While deeply lost in self-realisation, I fell asleep and in that state I had an experience of bliss in the company of my spiritual master.

Says Jñāneśvara, I am concerned with the almighty Paramātman. The brightness of His form shines forth everywhere. (679)

## 72

I am seized with a great longing for the Lord and my condition has just become like that of water feeling itself thirsty! I drank enough, but my thirst still remains unquenched.

Again and again I yearn to see king Viṭṭhala. Applying, therefore, the collyrium of devotion, I behold the purest Paramātman.

Thus, I see my own treasure. I have placed my grievance before Nivṛttinātha about this.

Says Jñāneśvara, a feeling of suffocation overtakes me if I forget to remember the feet of this Rakhumādevi's consort, father Viṭṭhala, even for a moment. (706)

## 73

With a mind full of devotion, I went to worship God when I experienced that I have myself become God!

I now do not see any dualism between God and His devotee which has disappeared just as salt is dissolved in the water of the sea!

I see God within and without everywhere and the concept of duality has become unbearable to me.

The Supreme Spirit which is present in the Ātman pervades all the animate and the inanimate creation.

Jñāneśvara says, since I have not invoked Him, how could He be forsaken? I shall humbly merge in Him. (713)

## 74

When you have attained the knowledge of self why should there be any misgiving in your mind? Are you still not freed from your ego?

Once you reach Him dispelling your ignorance, no such misgiving would ever bother you.

Why should you be obsessed with the fear of death when you have imbibed the nectar?

You will truly be happy when you eschew even the idea that you are the witness to whatever you perceive.

Says Jñāneśvara, Nivṛttinātha said to me, 'O Jñāneśvara listen! Once you relinquish your ego, you will know that you are none else but God Himself!' (716)

## 75

Like a river in spate, the entire sky was overflowing with the being of the Paramātman and the person witnessing the view was himself drowned in it!

The waves of the Paramātman who is the very life of all beings in this universe appear as those of the deluge coming at the time of the universal destruction.

Or it seems, the sky is all strewn over with pearls which are beyond anybody's reach.

The state of salvation should be experienced in this body itself by understanding the secret of self-realisation as unfolded by the spiritual preceptor.

Says Jñāneśvara, this Nivṛtti, the Munificent, after thoroughly convincing me showed this form of the Supreme Spirit to me. (720)

**76**

Now in this body itself, I have reached a state of bodilessness having freed myself of all the bonds of worldly life. It is all that now remains of me.

We are now our own Gods and are also our own devotees and have now been liberated from the bonds of worldly existence.

We shall now meditate only on ourselves and attain spiritual knowledge.

Fortunately, we have come to possess the expedient of repeating the prayer 'I am He!'

Says Jñāneśvara, I see the fascinating image of the Nirguṇa Paramātman in this form only. (723)

**77**

When the sun rises in the east, the lotuses bloom, but when it sets in the west and the moon rises, the lotuses contract.

Similarly, when the beloved sun of the Ātman rises, the lotus of the heart blooms. That which was far away now appears to be near!

Even though the moon is up in the sky in both the fortnights, it affects the sea by causing the ebb and flow on it. At Amāvāsyā, its disc is devoid of all brightness. The Ātman is similarly related to the body.

When clouds crowd together in the sky, peacocks start dancing on the earth. When the moon shines with its cool rays, the 'Cakoras' feel delighted.

When the sun is in the 'Svātī Nakṣatra' the pearl-producing shells receive its drops. Should the rain during other Nakṣatras be considered as unsalutory?

Says Jñāneśvara, the 'Cakora' broods over the moon as it fulfils its desires. Likewise, this Rakhumādevī's Lord, father Viṭṭhala has been held by me in my heart. (729)

**78**

The root of this tree is upwards in the unmanifest Brahman with its branches downwards in the animate and the inanimate creation which is manifest. Such a tree is found everywhere in the woods of the worldly life.

These trees have branches and sub-branches of the three Guṇas—Sattva, Rajas and Tamas, and yield numerous leaves and flowers.

Knowledge of self is the fruit thereof and the realisation—"I am Brahman" is its sweetness. On tasting this sweetness, a person feels gratified.

Says Jñāneśvara, the tree has grown up fully out of the seed of knowledge. (763)

**79**

Whose is the form which a human being possesses? Whose is the body? The Ātman knows this all.

Only during his life time a man should seriously think over the questions—'who am I?' and 'who are you?', and should endeavour to realise fully Govinda residing within his body.

This Paramātman transcends the triad—the 'object of meditation, the meditator and the meditation." He is more effulgent than the sun who shines forth with thousands of his rays.

Says Jñāneśvara, know the power of visualization which is in your eyes is the Brahman itself! (774)

**80**

To give the lioness's milk secured after great efforts, to a cat to drink. To acquire the unique knowledge of making a dead man alive and then for testing it to cut off one's own head!

To use a lamp for lighting several lamps and then to put out all of them!

To acquire a Philosophers' Stone and use it as an ordinary stone in the construction of a wall and to move about carrying in hand an ordinary stone!

To intentionally spill the nectar from a vessel and then to fill it with sour gruel!

Just as these are all foolish things, says Jñāneśvara, in the same way, the life of a person will be futile if he does not use the body obtained by him with a rare fortune, for realising God. (842)

**81**

Those who say they would get salvation after death are really great fools. Where is the light after the lamp is extinguished? How could then the things in a house be set in order?

Therefore, so long as your body is alive, strive to utilise it as a means of self-realisation and final beatitude.

Till the house is not fully burnt, extinguish the fire by pouring water on it. What is the use of pouring water after the entire house is burnt?

Says Jñāneśvara, I, the disciple of Nivṛttinātha, am exhorting you to know first who you are. (844)

**82**

Beware before death overtakes you and discover your own treasure—the realisation of self.

You are totally duped if you say you will follow some path of God-realisation in your old age—in the last days of your sojourn in this world?

If you consider your mortal body as immortal, the messengers of Yama will not fail to punish you.

Know well that the body is a food of the god of death. Bear, therefore, no fond affection for it.

In this life itself you stand to acquire a valuable treasure of self-realisation. Make, therefore, a sincere effort to accomplish it and benefit yourself.

This human body has been bestowed on you by God with rare fortune which you may not obtain again. Make, therefore, a determination today only to attain a state of intimate union with your deity.

Jñaneśvara says, contemplate over the question, 'who you are' or else lead the life of a stone! (845)

**83**

Know that one who is born as a human being but keeps himself away from devotion to God is truly a burden to the earth. His life is wasted and he can be compared only to a beast. How can a person swim across the sea of worldly life if he does not utter the name of Śrī Hari?

The tongue which forgets to utter the name of Śrī Hari, is like a frog indulging in prating. A man is sure to miss the way to Viṣṇu's abode (salvation) if he does not utter Hari's name.

Says Jñāneśvara, have full faith in the consort of Rakhumādevi, father Viṭṭhala. The entire movable and immovable world has survived only because of the remembrance of God's name. The name of Rāma-Kṛṣṇa alone is a true protector of all the human beings! (846)

**84**

Why unnecessarily mortify your body outwardly when the evil desires of your mind have not been subdued? While closing your eyes and holding your nose, please, do not brood over sensual pleasures, like a crane which appears to be standing in meditation near the bed of a river but is really intent on searching for fish!

For this, first cleanse your mind and heart. Renounce all your sensual desires. Forsaking your wife and children, you take refuge in a forest, but there also you remember your wife all the while. Of what avail then is the penance?

You may bathe in the waters of holy places even thrice a day, but how can you get rid of the impurities of your mind? On the contrary, these holy places will be defiled by your blemishes, and you will really become as impure as a washerman's stone!

Says Jñāneśvara, now whatever you have to do, do it with a clean mind. Your mind will alone be a witness to it. If you deceive people under one pretext or another, you will be forsaking God. My friend! for the sake of father Viṭṭhala, the consort of Rakhumādevī, please abstain from such a deceitful course.(852)

**85**

If you think of leaving your house as worthless, how are you going to get rid of the load of your body which is with you? If you consider your parents as bad and think of forsaking them, even then the problems of ego and ignorance will be with you! If you decide to renounce your real brothers, passions, anger, pride and envy will be with you as your brethren! If you think of forsaking your younger sister, hope, desire and illusion will still be there to vex you!

If this is the fact, please tell me what is it that you have really forsaken. The things dreading which you retire to the forest will be still with you accompanying your mind.

If you say that your wife is worthless, you have with you a wife in the form of your imagination which is capable of making you enjoy whatever you may desire. If you decide to renounce your children, you have not freed yourself from the pleasures of your senses. If you think of forsaking all your relatives, the eight-fold nature is already with you. If you decide to renounce all, you will lose your peace of mind.

When all this retinue is with you, why superficially shave your head and mortify your body? Reconciling yourself to whatever calamities that may befall you according to your fate or past deeds, remain in bliss which is so easy of achievement. Know well this secret of the teaching of your spiritual preceptor.

Says Jñāneśvara, those who follow and discharge the duties of their Āśrama, stand to get salvation. Rakhumādevī's consort, father Viṭṭhala will take them to the abode of Viṣṇu. (857)

## 86

When we gain something, we feel delighted. When we lose anything we feel unhappy. When we expend, our mind is worried over the expenditure. When all these fluxes and refluxes of the worldly life are agitating your mind, what is use of taking to renunciation by getting your head shaved? Has not a dextrous disguiser enough dresses and equipment at his disposal?

Therefore, first subdue the passions of your mind and then only take to renunciation by wearing a Sannyāsin's garments and adopting his way of life. Else, the path of renunciation becomes a mockery. Can anyone be purged of his blemishes only by begging? If this be so, does not a washerman beg on the day of a festival? Because of the Sannyāsin's outward attire that you have put on, people may give respect and you too may be puffed up with pride. But you fool! you will surely be duped.

By putting on a tattered robe, do you think you would be immune from the fear of death or that you would not be bound by your actions? Consider seriously what a true Yogī is like. Since his heart is as pure as a crystal, like a pure object matching with any sort of thing whatsoever into whose contact it comes, his purity of mind remains unaffected under any situation. He has no ill will towards any being and behaves alike to men of good and evil repute.

If your heart has not attained similar purity, do you think your simply putting on outwardly a Sannyāsin's attire and frowning on people with an air of authority or smearing sacred ashes on your body, could afford you any protection? Will it do you any good? You fool! Does not an ass roll on a heap of refuse to its heart's content? Does it do so at somebody else's bidding? By constructing a big monastery, you have indeed incarcerated yourself in it and have missed the right path.

Says Jñāneśvara, even if you visit a number of places of pilgrimage, do penance, bathe several times, meditate, or follow many such practices, be sure, you have missed the path of God-realisation. Purifying therefore, your mind first, concentrate it on the feet of Śrī Nivṛttinātha and go on uttering the name of

Viṭṭhala. Otherwise, you will fall into the snare of the worldly life for nothing. (859)

87

Ears, nose, tongue, skin and eyes are nothing else but the doors leading to wretchedness and misery. When the objects enjoyed by them do not give them pleasure, how can they give it to you? Therefore, think seriously on how best to obtain real happiness.

O mind, never forsake the lotus-feet of Śrī Hari.

Wealth possessed in a dream is no wealth at all. Water which is apparent in a mirage is no real water. The shadow of a cloud is not a real protection from the sun's heat. Considering all this, try to do whatever is expedient to understand your own Self as speedily as you can.

Says Jñāneśvara, why do you not realise Śrī Hari to whom you belong and in fact owe your very existence?

Fix your mind on the spouse of Rakhumādevī, father Viṭṭhala. Only then you will be able to realise Śrī Hari who is a repository of all happiness. (864)

88

Pleasures enjoyed in a dream are not real. Likewise, are the pleasures derived from the senses. If these are considered to be real, it would mean putting an end to one's life by swallowing poison!

Therefore, why waste your precious life for nothing? This mid-day shadow will disappear within no time. Considering therefore, that death may pounce upon you any time, devote yourself forthwith to worshipping Śrī Hari. You will then attain the abode of Viṣṇu quickly.

Jñāneśvara says, this Rakhumādevī's Lord, father Viṭṭhala standing on a brick has illumined the hearts of all beings with the light of His knowledge. (869)

89

The scented camphor disappears when burnt. A fly, then, is not attracted towards it.

The nose loves to smell a scented flower. A dark-blue bee likes to make a humming sound and, therefore, revolves around flowers.

A Rājahansa loves to feed on pearls. How can other birds, whose natural diet is different—not pearls, have a taste for them?

Says Jñāneśvara, they are truly wise who realise God in the embodied beings. Others have to be the guests of death! (871)

### 90

Is it not a futile exercise to try to catch fish in a mirage? Where is the water there and where is the fish?

Why indulge in a futile endeavour? How can you smell the flowers of the sky with your head?

How can you kill the son of a barren woman? When the child itself does not exist, how can you kill it?

Who is the soldier whom you would bring to ride a horse of clay? And whom would you conquer?

Says Jñāneśvara, why indulge in such futile ostentations? Better seek refuge at the feet of Śrī Nivṛttinātha. (876)

### 91

After a man is born in this world, what makes him his own enemy, is his ego which makes him think only in terms of his self and his body. He comes to feel an attachment towards his son, his wife and his wealth which acts as an impediment in his way of realising God. But he behaves like this without understanding that all these are but a prey of the god of death. Just as a man of confused thinking tied down by passion, anger, pride and envy does not recognise himself, even so, he is unable to know his Self. Just as a parrot, even when free, is not inclined to leave the rotating rod on which it rests, similarly, the Self, even though it is free, does not get rid of worldly attachments and allurements.

A fish in water being enticed by the bait, gets stuck to the hook and then moans due to excessive pain. Likewise, sensual pleasures appear very delightful in the beginning but when a person has to swallow their bitter fruits, he is visited with grief.

Just as the blowing of ash is not helpful in lighting a lamp, even so, the knowledge of Self cannot be gained by indulging in dry polemics over the dots and dashes of the Śāstras!

With the sole object of winning their bread, people who resort to austerity, penance, charity, pilgrimage and worship do only fruitless toil!

If a thirsty man runs after a mirage, he is deluded as he does not get the water of Gaṅgā to drink. Similarly, sensual pleasures do not eventually lead to happiness. But the pity is, even after undergoing lot of sufferings, a man does not become wiser.

Jñāneśvara says, a man who pursues sensual pleasures desperately without casting even a glance at his real happiness, falls into the widespread net of births and deaths. If a man continues his efforts to know his Self during his several births, only then will he qualify himself to realise the Paramātman. (881)

## 92

A big fair of the worldly life is held here. There is a bazar in this fair where ego, passion, anger, pride and envy are kept on sale. The result is, true religion has become extinct, while the trade in unrighteousness is thriving on briskly.

In this fair of the world, human beings having forsaken the Paramātman, are seen caught up in the snare of sensual pleasures.

Some are rejoicing in exhibiting their ego. Some have unpacked the bundles of self-conceit on the thoroughfare itself! Some are carrying their fame on donkeys. Still their desires remain unquenched.

Someone, who is learned, takes pride in exhibiting his erudition; some earn their bread by selling knowledge; and some take to the reading of Vedas simply to justify killings in the performance of sacrificial rites. Thus, in this congregation, millions of lives are toiling hard in furtherance of their selfish ends.

A huge quantity of the bags of ignorance is stored here. People are found going in for bad stuff in preference to things of good quality. So much are they after worldly pleasures that rejecting the nectar they are swallowing poison!

There is no place for kindness, peace or forgiveness in their hearts; and they are too much devoted to sensual pleasures. Though God is with them, they wander fruitlessly all the world over in His search. Forsaking their own religion, they embrace other religions.

Thus being thoroughly engrossed in the bazar, they have become completely oblivious of their real interests. They have misconceived the mortal body as Ātman and content themselves in swimming in deep waters of the mirage of worldly pleasures!

Says Jñāneśvara, but the wonder is, that Śrī Nivṛttīnātha has saved me from this predicament. He has transformed my looking at the world into non-looking by changing my mundane outlook into one of complete detachment from worldly affairs and thereby made me experience that the entire universe is pervaded by the Paramātman! This Lord of Rakhumādevī, father Viṭṭhala, has in His mercy revealed that God abides in me and that I am an indivisible part of this universe. (884)

## 93

Numerous birds from various islands gathered at the foot of the mountain Merū. Believing the white crystal-like rock, which lay there, to be a precious stone, they flew towards it.

The Rājahaṁsas tried their beaks on the rock. But when the beaks got entangled in the aperture of the rock, the Rājahansas realised their mistake.

Says Jñāneśvara, the learned are likewise duped when they keep company with the fool and lose remembrance of Lord Śrī Kṛṣṇa. (886)

## 94

God being formless, we are unable to see Him; whereas whatever is perceived by our senses does not correspond to His form. The days, thus, roll by witnessing creation and doom. Even when you know all this, you are not getting rid of the misconception of your mind. You do not maintain equanimity. Undoubtedly, this would not serve your interests.

Forsake therefore, illusion, temptation, strife and false hope. The thing of which you are in pursuit, will, in truth ultimately lead you to affliction.

Wealth possessed in a dream is not real wealth. A mirage is not real water. The shadow of clouds is not permanent but only transitory. Likewise, O my friend! sensual pleasure is not a real pleasure.

An elephant meets his doom by his craving for touch, a moth by its fascination for the glazing sight, a deer by its love for sound, a bee by its fondness for scent and a fish by its temptation for taste. The beings, thus, meet with a catastrophe due to these five objects of the senses. And understand well that you are closely encircled by all these five objects. How then do you expect that they would do you any good?

Does camphor ever emit any soot? Still you are out to paint the sky with it! It means, you are burning the camphor unnecessarily. The camphor will be wasted without giving you any soot and your indulgence will prove to be only a futile exercise. Whom then would you blame for your worries?

Says Jñāneśvara, the body for which you have so much affection stands grabbed by death since its very inception. In the face of all this, how do you not feel ashamed to indulge in an idle prate about 'I' and 'mine'? Therefore, please do not do like this. Instead seek refuge in Śrī Nivṛttinātha. This Rakhumādevī's Lord, father Viṭṭhala, will alone lead you ashore through the ocean of this worldly life. (887)

## 95

Believing the wealth possessed in a dream as real, you are embarking on business. But, where the principal itself does not exist, what to speak of any interest to accrue from it? You are running in pursuit of wealth and thus wasting your whole life in vain. In truth, you have been duped at the very moment you were born. Why then do you allow yourself to be duped again by believing your worldly pursuits as real and lasting?

Are you deceiving others or are you yourself being duped?

By ignoring your Ātman, you have destroyed the grandeur of your life. With whom are you now going to lodge a complaint?

Earth, water, splendour, air and the sky (space) have wrought this body of yours. By putting it to ceaseless toil, what is the wealth that you have accumulated? Think over this and you will come to realise that you have, in truth, extinguished the very light of your Ātman!

Says Jñāneśvara, you take pleasure in seeing your son, wife and wealth, but you do not realise that all of them are going to pass away like clouds which do not stay in the sky for long. With Rakhumādevī's Lord, father Viṭṭhala abiding in your heart, why do you get yourself ensnared in this mundane life? (889)

## 96

To undertake journey in the company of thieves is fraught with great risk.

Those who desire to tread on the path of the realisation of Brahman along with passions, anger and greed are fools indeed.

A man, intending to swim across the ocean with a stone tied to his neck, must be considered stupid for he would soon be drowned.

Forsaking, therefore, attachment for your house or your body, set out to seek the knowledge of the Supreme Spirit by following the purest means.

Says Jñāneśvara, if this is done, only then you can attain self-realisation; else your life will go astray. (894)

## 97

A fox howls so long as it does not face a lion.

A man's talk of renunciation lasts till a beautiful woman does not come in his sight! Friendship lasts so long as pecuniary dealings do not take place.

The war-cry continues till the enemy does not show himself to fight.

The sea goes on roaring till it has not seen the sage Agasti.

Jñāneśvara says, O brother! worldly calamities would continue to afflict you till you have not seen Rakhumādevī's Lord, father Viṭṭhala. (895)

98

Since the Paramātman is abiding in your heart, why do you serve this lifeless stone? What good will it bring to you?

O fool! Instead of realising the Paramātman who is the very source of all the places of pilgrimage, why are you labouring under a misconception that by visiting the places of pilgrimage you stand to get salvation?

Truly speaking, Lord Śrī Hari at whose feet lie one hundred and eight holy places has his abode in the temple of your heart in the form of your Ātman!

Says Jñāneśvara, when God is within you, why do you strive to visit the places of pilgrimage? If you do so, you will be missing the true reality itself. (903)

99

With a rare fortune, a man has been endowed with a body which is like a lustrous pearl. It alone is capable of making you realise the Paramātman.

What would you do if the treasure of self-realisation is lost? What is the use of repenting after the hand is burnt?

If after having taken a meal of ambrosia, you are required to wash your mouth with sour gruel, how greatly agitated you would feel? But then nothing can be done.

Says Jñāneśvara, so long as death does not claim you, take refuge at the feet of Rakhumādevī's consort, father Viṭṭhala. (906)

100

If good sugar is thoroughly mixed up with camphor, the mixture retains the aroma of camphor and the sweetness of sugar.

In the same way, by keeping close association with the

Paramātman who is different from your Jīvātman, try to be one with Him. This unity will open the gates of ecstatic joy for you.

Even if there exists a single sandal tree amidst other trees, the adjoining trees and plants become scented.

Says Jñāneśvara, if such unity takes place, Rakhumādevī's spouse, father Viṭṭhala who is most compassionate towards all beings, will never forsake them. (907)

**101**

A potter while preparing a pot goes on rotating his wheel. Likewise, O Lord! how long are thou going to revolve us?

To yearn for thee in this cycle of days and nights, is like lighting the wick of a lamp in a violent storm.

Says Jñāneśvara, this mundane life is nothing else but an unending mirage! Withdraw, therefore, your mind from it and fix it on the Paramātman. (917)

**102**

Though it is true that a cloud is the fountain of life for a 'Cātaka', it is on very rare occasions that its desire is fulfilled.

Similarly, a sun-nurtured lotus does not get the sun's benefit for all the time.

The 'Cakora' gets the advantage of the moon only on the full-moon night. For the rest of the days, it has to bear separation!

Likewise, to come to possess the body of a human being is a very remote possibility, but you have been fortunate enough to have it.

Says Jñāneśvara, you should, therefore, not forget Rakhumādevī's Lord, father Viṭṭhala even for a moment. (918)

**103**

The sky is studded with stars appearing as small and big lamps. There are millions of celestial bodies in the sky shining feebly as a moon. But their light is not capable of dispelling the darkness of the night. That act is accomplished only by the sun.

Likewise no salvation is possible without the grace of Śrī Gopāla. Even if you move all your life around a city, you cannot enter it unless you are able to find out its gate. Similarly, you will not get salvation unless you take refuge at the feet of Nanda's son, Lord Śrī Kṛṣṇa.

A body may be very handsome, but if it is lifeless, what is its use? Fie on the audience and orators who ignoring Lord Viṭṭhala, indulge in trivial talk!

Just as a body, bereft of its head, looks frightful or a river, without water, appears dreary or the sky in the absence of the sun or the moon seems gloomy, even so, a man's life too is meaningless unless he seeks refuge at the feet of Śrī Hari.

A man may be the lowest of the low, but if his heart yearns for Lord Śrī Kṛṣṇa, the spouse of Rukhmiṇī, he will not be bound by the ties of this worldly life. And even if a man be of a high caste or be a great ascetic, he will never be able to swim across the ocean of this worldly life if he does not fix his mind on Lord Śrī Kṛṣṇa.

There are numerous eye-like spots on the plumage of a peacock, but these are of no use since they lack vision ! Similarly, empty clouds crowding the sky are of no avail. All your actions are likewise fruitless unless you worship Śrī Kṛṣṇa, the Protector of Gokula.

Restraint, religious austerities, Prāṇāyāma and self-control are no doubt fruitful for the realisation of God, but so long as Lord Śrī Kṛṣṇa who is dark-blue as clouds and Tamāla in complexion is not firmly set in your heart, all these remedies may prove harmful.

So long as a person regards himself as superior to others and condemns them as insignificant and thus harbours in his mind anger and envy, his actions would lead him to misery only, and never to happiness.

Says Jñāneśvara, with the grace of Śrī Guru Nivṛttinātha, I have attained perfect unity with Rakhumādevī's Lord, father Viṭṭhala. (920)

## 104

O the dark-blue bee of my self! Forsake your blemish of unsteadiness and rejoice in the sweet scent of the petals of the lotus-feet of Lord Śrī Kṛṣṇa with a steadfast mind.

Enjoy this sweet scent of the flowers with a pure mind.

Says Jñāneśvara, this Rakhumādevī's Lord, father Viṭṭhala is the very incarnation of bliss and auspiciousness. Therefore, O my mind! take refuge at His feet. (926)

## 105

This Ātman is here, it is there; it is far off and it is in your house too. In fact, it pervades the entire universe!

Regard this whole visible world to be a Vivarta—an unreal and illusory form of the Supreme Spirit. Only then the divine discus of Lord Viṣṇu will spontaneously arrive at your cottage and whirl around it for your protection.

A swan is said to be capable of taking out milk separately from the admixture of milk and water. Likewise, a man of spiritual knowledge, sorts out things leading to the realisation of God from the transient affairs of this world.

Says Jñāneśvara, avoiding dry polemics on Śāstras I have merged in the form of the Paramātman. (944)

## 106

When you have been gifted with a priceless gem in the form of this human body, why do you not try to recognise the Paramātman who is the very source of this universe?

If you gain this knowledge, you will not get drowned (swim safely across) in the ocean of worldly life. As this knowledge (of the self) is difficult of attainment and beyond the comprehension of common men, there is no fear of its being robbed of. Therefore, O brother! clever as you are, acquire this knowledge.

Jñāneśvara says, I have gained this perennial knowledge of the Ātman from my spiritual preceptor. (971)

### 107

Why are you so much keen to have the view of the Paramātman? As He is formless, you will not be able to see Him. Instead, concentrate on realising your own self.

Once the knowledge of the self is attained, speech comes to an end and words fade away. A state of speechlessness comes to exist whilst you are in communion with the speechless Ātman!

Says Jñāneśvara, once a person comes to realise Rakhumādevī's spouse, father Viṭṭhala by the grace of his spiritual preceptor, words fail him and he experiences a state of speechlessness! (976)

### 108

We are the pilgrims. As a result of our pilgrimage, sins that beset us are taking to their heels in all directions.

We are the pilgrims of Paṇḍharpūra, and are proceeding northwards on our pilgrimage. See! the dawn of self-realisation has appeared today for we are happy to have the saints in our midst.

We are carrying the 'Kāvaḍa' of equality on our shoulders which is filled with the nectar of God's name. We have, as a result, been freed from the cycle of births and deaths. The entire atmosphere is profusely filled with the ecstatic joy of self-realisation.

There is now no need to mortify our bodies for attaining spiritual knowledge. Nor is there any necessity to shave our heads. The utterance of God's name will enable us to escape the contamination of our worldly actions.

Says Jñāneśvara, with the grace of Rakhumādevī's consort, father Viṭṭhala, we have been relieved of all our woes. (1058)

### 109

O Lord Śrī Kṛṣṇa! may thy image always abide in my heart.
May my eyes always love to see thy image.
May the wealth of utterance of thy name be always contain-

ed in my tongue. It is because of this keen desire that thy name has greatly fascinated me. With the ceaseless craving for this name in my heart, may I never forget thee.

May thou create in my mind such a liking for thee that my ears would always crave to hear thy sweet name.

By constant meditation on the Ātman, may thy Saguṇa form abide in my heart for ever! May I always long for thee. May my mind always contemplate on thee and my eyes always pine to see thy Saguṇa form. O the benevolent one! I entreat thee to relieve me from this unending cycle of births and deaths.

Says Jñāneśvara, O Rakhumādevī's Lord, father Viṭṭhala! It is only our devotion for thee that has enabled us to realise thee. Even the Purāṇas and the Śrutis describe thy glory by saying 'not this, not this!' Therefore, O the unparalleled One! O Nārāyaṇa! Give us always the pleasure of meditating on thy enchanting sweet name. (1098)

**110**

O Lord Śrī Kṛṣṇa! Just as a dark-blue bee is attracted towards a flowery creeper, may my mind always rejoice in meditating on thee.

Thy form is so fascinating that I never feel like withdrawing my eyes from it. But alas! thou dost not meet me even though thou art so close to me!

Just as thirst drives one to water, even so may my mind always pine for thee.

Says Jñāneśvara, since we are deeply attached to the consort of Rakhumādevī, father Viṭṭhala, the sweetness of our affection has mingled with the sweetness of our devotion for Him! (1100)

# EPILOGUE

*At the end of Jñāneśvarī, his famous Marathi commentary on the Bhagavadgītā, Śri Jñāneśvara invokes the Lord of the Universe to bestow on him the following benediction:*

Now the Paramātman who is the soul of this universe may be pleased with this literary sacrifice of mine, and bestow on me this blessing.

May the wicked be freed of their crookedness and may there arise in them a liking for benevolent acts, and may a sense of friendship prevail among all the beings.

May the darkness of sin disappear, may the world witness the rise of the sun of righteousness and may good desires of all the beings bear fruit.

May the congregation of the God's devotees engaged in showering on the earth all that is auspicious, meet all beings. These saints are like moving orchards of wish-trees, living mines of wish-jewels and conversing seas of nectar.

May virtuous people, who are like spotless moons or suns without their scorching splendour, evoke warm affection from all. In short, may all the three worlds be happy and keep themselves engaged in ceaseless worship of the all-sustaining Lord of the Creation.

And in particular, may those who regard this work as their sustainer, triumph over the visible and the invisible.

Whereupon Sadguru Nivṛttinātha was pleased and said, 'Amen! So be it!' On hearing this, Śrī Jñāneśvara became happy.

# GLOSSARY

*Abhaṅga*: A particular form of poetical composition (A devotional lyric). The popular metre used by many of the poet-saints in Marathi language.

*Agasti*: Name of a celebrated Ṛṣi or sage.

*Amāvāsyā*: Fifteenth day of the dark half of every lunar month.

*Āśrama*: The dwelling place of saints or religious devotees.

*Ātman*: The Self or Soul; denotes also the supreme Soul which according to Non-dualistic Vedānta is one with the individual soul.

*Bhagavadgītā*: A well-known Hindu scripture comprising eighteen chapters (25th to 42nd) of the Bhīśma Parva of the Mahābhārata.

*Brahman*: The Supreme Spirit. The one eternal principle in which all things exist.

*Bhajana*: Verses sung in worship by a group of persons collectively.

*Bhakti*: The worship of God expressed by loving devotion and reverence. It implics sincerity and purity of heart towards God.

*Bhaktimārga*: The way of bhakti; Securing of deliverance from rebirths by throwing oneself upon God's mercy, asking forgiveness for sins and thus securing God's free gift of salvation. A process that involves a change of heart and moral purity.

*Cakora*: A fabulous bird; the Greek partridge (said to feed on moon beams).

*Cakravāka*: The ruddy goose.

*Cātaka*: Name of a bird which is supposed to live only on rain drops.

*Cintāmaṇi*: A fabulous gem supposed to yield to its possessor all his desires.

*Dvārakā*: A city said to have been built by Viśvakarman. The capital of Ānarta. It sank into the sea after the death of Kṛṣṇa.

*Gangā*: The most sacred river in India and the deity presiding over it.

*Ghī*: Clarified or melted butter, used in cooking and in worship.

*Govinda*: A name of Śrī Kṛṣṇa.

*Guṇa*: An ingredient or constituent of nature; any one of the three properties belonging to all created things. (These are: Sattva, Rajas and Tamas).

*Guru*: A spiritual preceptor; a religious teacher.

*Japa*: The repetition of the name of God. Generally a rosary is used when God's names are repeated.

*Jīvanmukta*: One enjoying liberation while living in the body.

*Jīvātman*: Personal self.

*Kalpataru*: A tree supposed to grant all desires; a wish-yielding tree.

*Karma*: Action in general; duty.

*Kāvada*: A sling; a kind of appliance, for supporting hanging weight (of pots of water etc.)

*Kṛṣṇa, Śrī*: An incarnation of God Viṣṇu whose life is given in the *Bhāgavata* and the *Mahābhārata.*

*Kusumbā*: A kind of narcotic.

*Mahābhārata*: A famous Hindu epic on the great Bharata war.

*Māyā*: Illusion. The concept that the world is Māyā or illusion or transient as compared with the Brahman or eternal reality.

*Meru*: Name of the mythical golden mountain referred to in Hindu mythology. It is supposed to support the three worlds.

*Mogarā*: A kind of jasmine flower.

*Mukti*: Final beatitude or emancipation; salvation. (Four kinds of Muktis are: Salokatā, Samipatā, Sarupatā and Sāyujyatā).

*Nakṣatra*: Lunar mansions or asterisms. (There are in all 27 Nakṣatras).

*Nirguṇa*: Without attributes and usually refers to the Brahman or eternal reality which cannot be described.

*Pāṇḍavas*: The five sons of Pāṇḍu, viz. Yudhiṣṭhira, Bhīma, Arjuna, Nakula and Sahadeva. The heroes of the Great

Bhārata war in which the Kauravas were killed.

*Paṇḍharī*: Another name of Panḍharpūra.

*Panḍharināṭha:* Lord of Panḍharpūra, viz. God Pāṇḍuraṅga or Viṭṭhala.

*Parisa*: Philosophers' Stone.

*Parmātman:* The Supreme Spirit.

*Pārvatī*: Daughter of King Himālaya and consort of Śiva; a manifestation of the Divine Mother.

*Prakṛti-Puruṣa*: Terms used in the Sāṅkhya Philosophical system. Prakṛti refers to primordial matter or nature and Puruṣa to the soul.

*Prāṇāyāma*: Control of the vital breath.

*Purāṇas*: Books of Hindu mythology.

*Rājahansa*: A flamingo (supposed to have the power of separating milk from the mixture of milk and water).

*Rāma, Śrī*: The hero of the *Rāmāyaṇa,* regarded by the Hindus as a Divine Incarnation.

*Sadguru*: Generally means the best teacher. One who is a true religious guide, a spiritual preceptor.

*Saguṇa*: Possessed of qualities or attributes.

*Samādhi*: Ecstasy, trance, complete concentration, communion with God.

*Samsār*: The affairs of this world. The cares and entanglements of this life.

*Śaṅkara*: A name of Śiva. The Destroyer God. The Third Person of the Hindu Trinity, the other two being Brahmā and Viṣṇu.

*Sanyāsin*: An ascetic; one who renounces all ties with this life to realise God.

*Śāstras*: Scriptures.

*Śruti*: Generally refers to the Vedas including Upaniṣads.

*Sukṛta:* Virtue, moral or religious merit.

*Tāmbula*: The leaf of piper-betel, which together with areca-nut, catechu, chewed after meals.

*Tapa*: Religious austerities practised in order to secure salvation.

*Tīrtha*: A sacred spot or a place of pilgrimage.

*Upaniṣad*: The last part of Śruti—Hindu philosophical literature greatly venerated.

*Upāsanā*: Service, worship.

*Vaikuṇṭha*: The abode of God Viṣṇu.

*Veda*: The oldest and the most revered of the Hindu scriptures. The four Vedas are the *Ṛg-Veda*, the *Yajur-Veda*, the *Sām-Veda* and the *Atharva-Veda*.

*Viṣṇu*: A name of the Supreme Lord, the Preserver God, the second Person of the Hindu Trinity, the other two being Brahmā and Śiva.

*Vivarta*: An apparent or illusory form; an unreal appearance caused by human error. (This is a favourite doctrine of the Vedāntins according to whom the whole visible world is a mere illusion, an unreal and illusory appearance while Brahman or Supreme Spirit is the only reality).

*Viṭṭhala*: Another name of Lord Pāṇḍuraṅga.

*Vyāsa*: A celebrated sage, who is reputed to have arranged the Vedas in their present form; he is also believed to be the author of the *Mahābhārata*, the eighteen Purāṇas, and the Brahma-sūtras.

*Yama*: The God, who rules over the regions where departed spirits have gone.

*Yoga*: The processs of seeking salvation by means of meditation and contemplation. Spiritual exercises.

*Yogin*: One who performs meditation or who is supposed to possess miraculous powers by the practice of Yoga.

# INDEX